Wings of the Morning

A Song in the Night

Natalie A. Pierce

PRESS

Wings of the Morning Psalm 139:9
A Song in the Night Psalm 77:6
by Natalie A. Pierce

Printed in the United States of America

ISBN 9781619967014

www.xulonpress.com

Dedication

❖

This book is dedicated to my children who have always been the joy of my life: Bob (Nancy) Pierce, Judy Bengar and Sue (Bill) Burton, and to my beloved grandchildren: Mike Roberts, Suzanne Nelson, James Burton, Michael Pierce, Laurie Vaughn, Andy Pierce, Beth Burton, Daniel and David Pierce; my eighteen great-grand children and one great-great-granddaughter.

Acknowledgments

I want to say a very special thank you to my dear family who have stood by me and encouraged me every step of the way.

I also want to thank all my brothers and sisters in Christ who have been so instrumental in helping me stay true to the course God has set before me

To all of those who have encouraged me and helped me to see the "Wings of the Morning - A Song in the Night" project come to fruition: Pastor (Dr.) Doug and Doris Jensen and Dr. John and Karen Knapp; I couldn't have done it without you.

Thank you Pam McLaughlin for your patience throughout the entire editing process.

Table of Contents

Introduction

"For the sake of Jacob My servant, And Israel My chosen one, I have also called you by your name; I have given you a title of honor, though you have not known Me."

(Isaiah 45:4 NAS)

Writing stems from a compulsion - a fierce necessity - of having to say something or having something to say. I've been bothered no end, wondering under which category this might fall. Having "succumbed" to the conclusion that this is a little of both, I am prepared to risk the consequences.

When the skies are blue, the meadows green, and the winds from the south blow softly, then my spirit soars on the Wings of the Morning. His hand leads me and holds me. I know it in my heart (see Psalm 139:9).

But when the darkness settles in, be it mid-morning or midnight, that's when I call to remembrance my Song in the Night. That's when I meditate within my heart and my spirit makes diligent search. That's when I get to know God better (see Psalm 77:6). That's when I dig for the treasures of darkness and hidden riches of secret places, that I may know Him better, who calls me by name (see Isaiah 45:4-5).

My prayer is that you may be blessed by the fruits of my search and come to know the One who made you and called you by name.

Intangible

Time is today and a host of yesterdays

The happiness and sorrows we have tasted;

We measure it by sun and moon

And a hundred other ways

Those precious moments some of us have wasted.

Time is life in essence – we borrow not nor lend it;

To love - to hate - to give - to get –

How shall we choose to spend it?

Acceptance

❖

"Oh, My Father, if this cup may not pass away from me, except I drink it, Thy will be done." (Matthew 26:42 KJV)

If we would learn about acceptance from the life of another, we might well focus on the life of Amy Carmichael, the young woman from Ireland who became a missionary to India during the 1890's. Her experience cancels out any idea that acceptance equals resignation, and gives added dimension for those who may be facing what appears to be a dead end. What the caterpillar calls an end, God calls a butterfly.

When she was a little girl, brown-eyed Amy had an insatiable yearning for blue eyes. Believing that God would answer her prayers, she prayed earnestly one night that He might change the color of her eyes. When she awoke the next morning, she hopped vigorously out of bed, and propped a stool up in front of her dresser. She excitedly climbed to where she could see in the mirror. She found to her utter dismay, brown eyes staring back at her from the mirror. She wept bitterly at the realization that God's answer sometimes comes in the form of "No." This was Amy's first real opportunity to "accept" disappointment in her life.

Many years later she was to learn the "why" of brown eyes. She was called of God to rescue precious little boys and girls from being sold or given for temple prostitution in Dohnavur, an obscure place tucked away in the south of India. She risked her life daily, hiding children and protecting them from the authorities. Time and again, garbed in a sari with darkened skin, she masqueraded as a native. Blue eyes would have made her mission literally impossible. God's purpose will not be thwarted, even though the answer is, "No".

After serving the Lord for more than 20 years, Amy had the misfortune of falling into an unmarked pit dug by construction workers. She suffered painful injuries from which she never recovered. Her last twenty years were spent as an invalid, confined for the most part to her bed in her beloved India. During those years, she continued as overseer of the work, but it is her writings which have since blessed and encouraged many generations of souls. On her sickbed, Amy's yielded spirit—her capacity to accept God's will—led to an enviable, intimate relationship with Him. Such inspired gems as "Rose from Briar," "Toward Jerusalem," and "Candles in the Dark," flowed from her pen. It was during this period that she wrote: "In acceptance lieth peace."

We will either **go** through life's hardships or **grow** through them. It has been said that life is not fair, but God is good. Once we have accepted this as a measuring stick, we are on the road to peace—not as prescribed by the world, but the peace that Jesus gives.

"Peace I leave with you; my peace I give to you; I do not give to you as the world gives. Do not let your heart be troubled, and do not be afraid." (John 14:27 NIV)

A House Like His

❖

"For our citizenship is in heaven, from which we also eagerly wait for theSavior, the Lord Jesus Christ, who will transform our lowly body that it may be conformed to His glorious body, according to the working by which He is able even to subdue all things to Himself." (Philippians 3:20-21)

How good can it get? Of all the promises of God to His children, the guarantee of a new "glorious" body like Jesus', one that offers freedom from pain and suffering, is probably the pledge that makes heaven most appealing. While it is true that we are fearfully and wonderfully made (see Psalm 139:14), time takes its toll on our "parts." We are not created to endure forever in these earthly "houses." Adam's sin nature, which we inherited, cancels out that option.

However, we *do* need to respect this "tent, tabernacle, temple" in which we live. We are admonished to abstain from sin and immorality because our bodies are "a temple of the

Holy Spirit who is in you, whom you have from God..." (1 Corinthians 6:19).

Remember the time Jesus drove the money changers out of the temple and the Jews asked Him for a sign to prove that He was who He claimed to be? Jesus, referring to His own body, answered and said to them, "Destroy this temple, and in three days I will raise it up" (John 2:12-21). So saying, He predicted what would happen after His crucifixion. His body which He referred to as this temple WAS raised up—one that appeared seemingly out of nowhere—to Mary. "Now the first day of the week Mary Magdalene went to the tomb early, while it was still dark, and saw that the stone had been taken away from the tomb. Then she ran to tell Peter and John... who checked the tomb and found it empty except for the linen cloths that had bound Him...After they left she stood, weeping, when Jesus appeared and called her by name, 'Mary!' " (John 20:1-19).

The Apostle Paul, writing to believers in Corinth, referred to our bodies as tents: "For we know that if the earthly tent which is our body is torn down, we have a building from God, a 'house' not made with hands, eternal in the heavens. For indeed in this 'house' we groan, longing to be clothed with our dwelling from heaven" (2 Corinthians 5:1-2 NAS). We are enlivened with the hope (an expected end) of giving up this earthly tent for a new "house," one "not made with hands," one like Jesus' eternal, heavenly body. Jesus' body would not "see corruption," as foretold in Old testament Scriptures Psalm 16:9-10 and Psalm 49:15.

"For I delivered to you… that Christ died for our sins according to the Scriptures, and that He was buried, and that He was raised on the third day according to the Scriptures, and that He was seen by Clephas (Peter), then to the twelve. After that He was seen by more than five hundred brethren at once, of whom the greater part remain to the present, but some have fallen asleep; then He was seen by James, then all the apostles. Then last of all, He was seen by me also, as by one born out of due time" (1 Corinthians 15:3-8). We can imagine the comfort and joy that Jesus, in His resurrected body, must have brought to those faithful followers. He had told His disciples that He would go and prepare a place that they might join Him. Then word came that Jesus had been crucified, died and was buried in the tomb of Joseph of Arimathea. Miracle of miracles, there He was in a glorified body, His eternal "house."

Often referred to as the "mystery of resurrection" is the revealing Scriptural account in 1 Corinthians 15:50, "I declare to you, brothers, that flesh and blood cannot inherit the kingdom of God; nor does the perishable inherit the imperishable nor corruption inherit incorruption" (NIV).

"Behold, I tell you a mystery; we shall not all sleep but we shall all be changed - in a moment, in the twinkling of an eye, at the last trumpet. For the trumpet will sound, and the dead will be raised incorruptible, and we shall be changed. For this corruptible must put on incorruption, and this mortal must put on immortality. So when this corruptible has put on incorruption, and this mortal has put on immortality, then shall be brought to pass the saying that is written, 'Death is swallowed up in victory. O death, where is your sting? O death, where is your victory?'…but thanks be to God, who gives us the victory through our Lord Jesus Christ. For the believer, death is an occasion to *celebrate* a new beginning. This should spur us on to be steadfast…always abounding in the work of the Lord, knowing that your labor is not in vain in the Lord." (1Corinthians 15:51-58)

Jesus appeared to His disciples behind closed doors (see John 20:19-23). Apparently, the molecules of His body were changed as ours will be. Our spiritual bodies will be unlike these earthly "houses." Jesus and the disciples recognized one another immediately and communication was no problem at all. He cooked a breakfast of fish and ate it with the disciples (see John 21:11-15). He joined a couple of them on the road to Emmaus, explained the Scriptures clearly to them, and after breaking bread, "vanished from their sight" (see Luke 24:13-35).

One day we will have an ethereal "house like His." We will pass through closed, locked doors. We will recognize one another and enjoy sweet fellowship as we break bread together. We will be rejoicing and worshiping God for all eternity! Doesn't that gladden your heart?

"Beloved, now we are children of God, and it has not yet been revealed what we shall be, but we know that when He is revealed, we will be *like* Him, for we will see Him as He is. And everyone who has this hope in him purifies himself, just as He is pure." (1 John 3:2)

A New Name

"…To him who overcomes…I will give him a white stone, and a new name written on the stone which no one knows but he who receives it." (Revelation 2:17 NAS)

Remember this old gospel song? "There's a *new name* written down in Glory, and it's mine; Oh! yes, it's mine." It's true. God's Word confirms it. "But now, thus says the LORD, who created you, O Jacob and He who formed you, O Israel: 'Fear not, for I have redeemed you, I have called you by *your name*; You are Mine' " (Isaiah 43:1). Just as He called Israel by its name, He has called each one of His children by his/her name. Furthermore, God's children are called by *His name* and He has created us for His glory (see Isaiah 43:7).

When God made His covenant with Abram, He changed his name to "Abraham," meaning "father of many nations." When Sara was about to fulfill that prophecy and bear Abraham a son, Isaac, she was given the name "Sarah," meaning "princess."

Changing names was the custom with any covenant at that time in history. It is believed that the "h" was added because it is affiliated with the name YAHWEH or YHWH, traditionally pronounced "Jehovah." People in third world countries today assume *new names* whereby they identify themselves with the Lord Jesus Christ when they become Christians.

For instance, one young Korean man named "Boohong" has become a pastor now called "Peter" (a stone); another man whose name was "Eunuk" is now called "Joseph" (increaser). Another changed his name to "Luke" (light giver). Youn, a young woman, has assumed the name "Grace." They have chosen new names to represent their new faith even though they risk prejudice and mockery from their country-men, who do not understand. They are *eager* to be known as *Christians.* Christians were first called "Christ-Ones" (deri-sively) at Antioch (see Acts 11:26). Tacitus, a first century writer, wrote: "The *vulgar* call themselves *Christians!*" They chose a *new name* when it was regarded in their culture as either highly irregular or downright disgraceful, and it often led to persecution.

A story quoted in the Multnomah Message relates how a man found a young eagle which had fallen out of its nest in the forest. He took it home and put it in his barnyard where it adopted the manner and behavior of his chickens. It did not learn to fly. A naturalist, believing that the bird had the *heart* of an eagle and could be taught to fly, made several attempts at lifting the eagle toward the sky, but the poor thing was confused. He did not know who he was. Finally, after he had gone back and forth from the chicken coop to a place of freedom a few times, the bird lover took him to a mountain, held him high, and aimed him straight toward the sun, reminding him, "You are an eagle. Stretch your wings and fly!" Slowly, the eagle stretched his wings and flew away triumphantly toward the sun, never to return to the barnyard. He had a *new name*; it was "eagle."

It is vital that we know who we are and behave accordingly. Regardless of our background, upbringing, past or present— Jesus Christ will take us to the mountain top where we may spread our wings as the eagle and begin life anew. Yes, we have a *new name* written down in Glory, but we don't need to wait—we can build upon the Christian name now! Our Korean friends know who they are and their desire is to measure up to their *new names.*

Oswald Chambers in, *My Utmost for His Highest*, writes: "the disciple is the one who has the *new name* written all over him; self-interest, pride and self-sufficiency have been completely erased."

How shall we be remembered? Will it be by the name "Christian"? Jesus prayed: "Holy Father, keep through *Your name* those whom You have given Me, that they may be one, as We are" (John 17:11).

"He who overcomes, I will make him a pillar in the temple of My God, and he will not go out from it anymore; I will write on him the name of My God…" (Revelation 3:12 NAS)

As the Eagle

✤

"As an eagle stirs up its nest, hovers over its young, spreading out its wings, taking them up, carrying them on its wings, so the Lord alone led him."

(Deuteronomy 32:11,12a)

H ave you ever experienced the rude awakening that occurs when you realize that your cozy nest is being "stirred up" and you find yourself teetering on the ragged edge, then plunging downward, leaving your comfort zone far behind, frightened at the uncertainties that lie ahead? God provides for the "birds of the air which neither sow nor reap" (Matthew 6:26), and He loves us "as a father pities his children" (Psalm 103:13), carrying us at times, as an eagle bears her young.

Eagles are mentioned thirty-eight times in the Scriptures, always for the benefit of teaching us a lesson. Eagles mate for life. They use the same nest for life, a nest that may range from nine to twenty feet in width. Parents share the responsibility of protecting their young, sitting on the eggs for at least one month. A mother eagle will stir up her nest and shove her eaglet out of it—at her discretion—when it is time for it to fly. She will soar, carrying the eaglet on her back, swoop down and let it fall; but if the youngster is not strong enough to fly, she will again swoop down underneath her charge and carry it on her wing, back to the safety of the nest. Occasionally, the fledgling will fly on its first try, but if not, the process is repeated until the lesson is complete. The young bird is never tested beyond its endurance. *Nor are we.*

We may be comfortable in our nest; unwilling to leave our secure place; afraid that we will fall, never to rise again. But God said: "You have seen what I did to the Egyptians, and how I bore you on eagles' wings and brought you to Myself. If you will indeed obey my voice and keep my covenant, then you shall be a 'special treasure' to Me above all people; for all the earth is Mine" (Exodus 19:4,5). How many times has God disarmed our enemy and drawn us to Himself? Our *"special treasure"* status guarantees His tender, loving care.

The eagle has magnificent powers of flight and vision. He can identify a rabbit moving about one mile away and can spot a six-inch fish that is two feet below the water, from a distance of up to two miles away. He travels alone and flies higher than most other birds, flying at forty-four miles per hour, but when propelled by a turbulent wind; he may glide at one hundred miles per hour. Their diving speed is estimated at seventy-five to one hundred miles per hour. Eagles can fly above the clouds to altitudes of ten thousand feet or more.

They will watch an approaching storm and when it strikes, they will *face it* and soar effortlessly into it, letting the wind carry them, where other fowl beat frantically with their wings to stay aloft. Eagles soar! When we sense danger lurking on our path, it is logical that we take steps to avoid harm. But there are times in the storms of life when no amount of "flapping our wings" is going to affect the outcome. Those are the occasions we need to let God carry us, enabling us to meet the challenge and soar above our predicament, *as the eagle.* Can we wait for God's "updraft" to lift us? If we will wait upon the Lord, He will empower us to 'soar' above the problem, to the place where there is safety in the storm.

Our Heavenly Father allows us to see beyond our circumstances, and through the power of the Holy Spirit, allows us to rise above the storm on wings of faith. Eagles have been given eyes that see great distances that can look directly into the sun and not be blinded. God has given us spiritual eyes to see the Son in our circumstances, eyes that can probe the nature of God, the depth of God and the love of God. "Those who wait on the Lord shall renew their strength; they shall mount up with wings like eagles" (Isaiah 40:31).

This magnificent bird lives an average of sixty years. In order to maintain good health, at about age thirty, an eagle must withdraw into a hiding place to "renew its strength." Out of its seven thousand feathers, it will pull out the soiled wing feathers – extract its calcified claws and smash its beak – a very painful process; leaving itself totally vulnerable. If it cannot complete the process, it will solicit the help of another eagle to do it. Then it waits, quite helpless for a time – later emerging in its renewed condition, stronger than before. It is vital that the eagle be renewed if it is to live a productive life. What about us? "Listen to your body," warns the doctor, "so you will know when to rest." Many of us have experienced enforced rest through illness or an accident, perhaps feeling that we have lost our purpose in life. But God has not forsaken us. He has a purpose for us.

"...For He Himself has said, 'I will never leave you, nor forsake you'" (Hebrews 13:5). We are told that in the original language, Hebrews 13:5 reads, "I will never, no never, no never – leave you or forsake you." We *will* be renewed, either in this life or when we join Jesus and our loved ones in eternity. Is it any wonder that God draws a parallel between us and this magnificent bird? The eagle is a perfect role model, becoming completely debilitated for a time, trusting God to renew its strength.

There are special periods when life is on hold; we are forced to pause, unable to perform. George Frederic Handel (1685-1759) had accommodated a hectic schedule for years to the point where he became exhausted, broken. He rested for a period of eleven months. Then one night he felt as though he had had a visitation from God. He arose from sleep and began feverishly writing music. Handle's burst of spiritual revival empowered him to write almost compulsively for 24 days, often refusing nourishment, until he completed the most famous sacred oratorio of all time, "The Messiah." God had compelled a great composer to rest for a season, as the eagle, so that with restored vitality His purpose might be accomplished.

"Bless the Lord, O my soul…who satisfies your mouth with good things, so that your youth is renewed like the eagles."

(Psalm 103:1, 5)

A Wardrobe for all Seasons

❖

"The Spirit of the Lord God is upon Me, because the Lord has anointed Me…to comfort all who mourn, to console those who mourn in Zion, to give them beauty for ashes, the oil of joy for mourning, the garment of praise for the spirit of heaviness.…" (Isaiah 61:1-3)

The veld in South Africa yields a lovely tale, a true story of "beauty for ashes." It gives added dimension to "burnt offerings" as it nourishes our desire for natural beauty. A veld is open country bearing mostly grass, along with a few scattered bushes and shrubs. Periodically, as ecology runs its course, fire breaks out and hundreds of acres of grassy plain and hills are burned to a crisp. What had been green mountains and valleys are suddenly blackened and covered with a layer of ashes. In a short time, however, as the green grass reappears, a little scarlet flower called the "fire lily" also makes it way through the ashes, dressing the landscape anew with cheery red blossoms. The fire lily is a perfect embodiment of "beauty for ashes."

From ashes to beauty – isn't it just like God to "draft" such a perfect plan? He has, in like manner, given His children a pattern which allows us to change from our old, drab apparel to a new and attractive *spiritual* wardrobe; one which is suitable for each season of life. First, comes the covering of salvation. Romans 13:12 warns us to "cast off your dark deeds like dirty clothes, and put on the shining armor of right living." Let us put on the armor of light (NLV).

We are to avoid such improper behavior as drunkenness, immorality, strife and jealousy; putting them off or laying them aside; as we would a worn out garment (see Romans 13:13). "Rather, *clothe yourselves* with the Lord Jesus Christ, and do not think about how to gratify the desires of the sinful nature" (Romans 13:14 NIV). Once we have "clothed ourselves" with or "put on" the Lord Jesus Christ surrendering our lives to Him, worldly pleasures will no longer have the same appeal to us that they once did. We will begin to experience the various phases or seasons of life on an entirely new level.

God has laid out a pattern for us to clothe ourselves with Christ. He tells us to "put off" or "lay aside" the old self with its deceit and corruption. Then we are to "put on" our new self which has been created in the likeness of God in righteousness and holiness. We are to lay aside falsehood, stealing, and vulgar language. All of the old bitterness and wrath which we have been harboring must be put away and replaced with kindness, forgiveness and compassion (see Ephesians 4:22-32).

The same issue—"taking off" or "laying aside" our old self with its evil practices and "putting on" the new man—is addressed in Colossians 3:1-13. "And above all these things *put on* love, which is the bond of perfection."

Peter reminds us to "be submissive to one another, and be *clothed* with humility" (1 Peter 5:5 emphasis added). We are to lay aside our pride in exchange for humility, which is more attractive anyway. When we do, our wardrobe takes on a whole new look and is appropriate for all seasons.

You may be in a spring season, enjoying the "more abundant life" that God intends for us as He reveals truths from His Word, blessing us day by day (John 10:10). Those are precious days as daffodils and tulips sprout up and shoot forth colors that take your breath away. Spring is the season of plenty and of rejoicing in the Lord (Philippians 4:4).

Conversely, you may find yourself temporarily in a season of darkness where storm clouds border your horizon, blotting out the sun. You may be enduring a broken relationship, loss of a job, or an illness, even a terminal illness. During this season of heaviness, God offers us a perennial spiritual wardrobe—"beauty for ashes, the oil of joy for mourning, and the garment of praise for the spirit of heaviness." Regardless of what lies over the horizon, when we offer up words of praise to God by putting on this garment of praise, He invariably lifts our thoughts and minds to a higher level because He *inhabits* our praise. "But You are holy, enthroned in the praises of Israel" (Psalm 22:3). "Great is the Lord and greatly to be praised in the city of our God, in His holy mountain" (Psalm 48:1). "In the courts of the Lord's house, In the midst of you, O Jerusalem, Praise the Lord" (Psalm 116:19). "Praise the Lord, all you Gentiles! Laud Him, all you peoples" (Romans 15:11). The garment of praise is becoming. We should wear it often.

We are assured that Christ became unto us "wisdom, righteousness, sanctification and redemption" (1 Corinthians 1:30). We are protected by His "cloak of righteousness" day after day, in all kinds of weather—in sunshine or in storm. It is that part of our wardrobe that shelters us at all times. It is unique because it is tailor made to fit each one of us. In "putting on" or "clothing ourselves" with the Lord Jesus Christ, we will be transformed like the fire lily in the African veld, creating "beauty for ashes" and "the *garment* of praise for the spirit of heaviness" (Isaiah 61:3).

Babe in the Manger

❖

"And the Word became flesh, and dwelt among us, and we beheld His glory, glory as of the only begotten from the Father,) full of grace and truth." (John 1:14)

Although the world about us is in turmoil as we approach this Holy-Day Season, much of our attention will center around the traditional Nativity Scene as it depicts the birth of a Savior. Jesus Christ was born approximately 2,000 years ago in a little village called Bethlehem. Tradition lends itself to the celebration of His birth on December 25, whereas it is likely that the Baby Jesus was born in the spring at the time of Passover and early harvest. We don't really know. There were two harvests at that time – one in spring and one in autumn. Since there was "no room for them at the inn," they were probably housed in a shelter that provided housing for beasts of burden by which patrons had traveled, and sometimes their owners as well. This would not have been a barn or a stable as we know it today, but it would resemble an old livery stable, replete with a feeding trough (manger) common to early America.

History tells us that back in the year 1223 A.D., St. Francis of Assisi created an enactment of the first nativity scene. It featured a "crèche" (the French word for "cradle") for Baby Jesus. It was replete with real animals and shepherds. People enacted the parts of Mary, Joseph and the Baby Jesus. A live ox and a donkey rounded out the display. St. Francis died before age fifty, leaving a tremendous legacy of wisdom, borne out in his writings. It is said that the birth of Christ was a "key component" of his spirituality. Isn't that true of all of us? It is the Reason for the Season, and without it there would have been no redemption for the believer on a hill called Calvary.

Gifts of Gold, Frankincense and Myrrh:

The Magi-Wise Men-probably consisted of a large band of men since it would have been prohibitive for a small group to traverse the highways safely at this time. They brought gifts of gold, frankincense and myrrh. Jesus was probably between six months and two years old when they arrived with their gifts.

1. **Gold**: The most precious of metals, signifying Deity. Hence, it was a logical love offering to the Christ Child.

2. **Frankincense**: Associated with prayer. Sometime in historic antiquity, men discovered that the burning of certain plants gave forth fragrant smoke. Frankincense is a sweet smelling aroma which delights the senses. Taken from the gum or resin of trees and shrubs found in southern Arabia, of the species "boswellia," it became very costly and brought wealth to those who had access to it. It was much sought after and soon became associated with kings and priests. It was more valuable in weight than gold. Frankincense speaks of the prayers of the saints, as they waft upward to God.

"Another angel came and stood at the altar, holding a golden censer and much incense was given to him, so that he might add it to the prayers of all the saints...And the smoke of the incense, with the prayers of the saints, went up before God out of the angel's hand" (Revelation 8:3,4 NAS).

3. **Myrrh**: Comes from the dried sap of a tree from Somalia and Ethiopia. It was extensively used in embalming, symbolic of the death that Jesus would suffer on the Cross. It is known to give off an earthy, bitter odor when burned, but develops a sweet scent when crushed. Bitterness crushed to become sweet. How prophetic. Jesus Christ would suffer the bitterness of our sins on a Cross at Calvary in exchange for the sweet fragrance of forgiveness.

Each gift bore an overtone of something sacred, offered *after* the Wise Men had fallen down and worshipped the King.

How shall we worship Him? What can we bring? Perhaps, we can offer a *heart* that is tender toward Him, ready to be filled with His love. Add to that, a *will* that is yielded to Him so that our members become instruments of His righteousness and finally, a *spirit* that is filled with Him so that He may sanctify us and make us fit for the Master's use.

It all began – the beginning of Christmas – on a star-lit night in a little town called Bethlehem, when "the Word became flesh and dwelt among us" – giving us the Reason for the Season. There is nothing "*seasonal*" however, about Jesus Christ or His Word. He is the same – yesterday, today and forever according to Hebrews 13:8. He is "the Alpha and Omega (beginning and end), Who is and Who was and Who is to come; the Almighty" as per Revelation 1:8. The nativity, a vital part of His story, gives us cause to pause and reflect. Our eternal destiny hinges on our relationship to the Babe in the Manger, the Christ-child, who would one day become our Savior - to redeem us from our sins.

"But you, Bethlehem, in the land of Judah, are not the least among the rulers of Judah; for out of you shall come a Ruler, who will shepherd my people Israel." (Matthew 2:6)

Broken Things

"And being in Bethany at the house of Simon the leper, as He sat at the table came a woman having an alabaster flask of very costly oil of spikenard. Then she broke the flask and poured it on His (Jesus) head." (Mark 14:3)

M ary of Bethany, the woman described in Mark 14, had an alabaster "box" also called a flask, probably an exquisitely carved receptacle, containing expensive perfume. Her treasure, however, was of no use to the kingdom until it was broken. Neither are we. Gideon was a man chosen by God to deliver Israel from the Midianites (Judges 7). He selected an army of three hundred men, each of which carried a trumpet in one hand and an earthen pitcher with a torch hidden inside in the other. The noise of the trumpets (signifying victory) and all those pitchers breaking, along with the sudden lighting up of the torches inside them, was intended to deceive the Midianites as to the size of Gideon's army. The plan worked. The enemy fled for cover as the lights shone in a blaze of glory—*after* the pitchers were broken. God uses broken things.

The word for "broken" in the case of the alabaster box—flask—vessel—implies something "shattered—broken to slivers." It was splintered beyond repair. Like Humpty Dumpty, all the king's horses and all the king's men could not put it together again. Only then could the spikenard (an expensive aromatic oil extracted from an East Indian plant) be spilled out in an act of worship. In like manner, it was necessary that the pitchers (man-made vessels) carried by Gideon's army, be dashed to pieces and shattered before they were of any use to God. However, He has devised quite a different plan for us, vessels *He* has created. We may be broken, but we will not be crushed.

> "For it is the God who commanded light to shine out of darkness, who has shone in our hearts to give the light of the knowledge of the glory of God in the face of Jesus Christ. But we have this treasure in earthen vessels, that the excellence of the power may be of God and not of us." (2 Corinthians 4:6-7)

Jars of Clay

The Apostle Paul says that we are perplexed, persecuted and struck down, but not destroyed. We, as earthen vessels, are broken for the express purpose of being renewed, refinished, and re-shaped. Why? That "the life of Jesus may be manifested in our bodies." It is only when others see Jesus in us that we glorify Him. We are called upon to be partakers of Jesus' suffering. "Though now for a little while, if need be, you have been grieved by various trials" (1 Peter 1:6), but we have God's promise that "after we have suffered a while," He will "perfect, establish, strengthen and settle" us (1 Peter 5:10). He will *perfect us* (fit together, as a dislocated joint or broken bone), the implication being that we will be stronger than ever. He will *establish* us (make fast, set, ground), lay a firm foundation, and gird us with His *strength* for the future. We need not fear the trial that is testing our mettle at the present time, though it is painful "for a while." Strength is perfected through brokenness. We are told in 1 Peter 4:12-13 not to think it strange concerning the fiery trial which is to try us as though some strange thing had happened to us. We should rejoice to the extent that we partake of Christ's sufferings, knowing that when His glory is revealed, we may also be glad with exceeding joy (paraphrased). This is not easy.

Paraplegic Joni Eareckson Tada, whose neck was broken in a swimming-diving accident, speaks from the vantage point of literal brokenness. She states unequivocally that her ministry among those with handicaps would never have materialized had she not suffered physical and emotional pain. Partially healed, she will always be dependent on others for many of the necessities of life. Yet as an ambassador for Christ, she inspires hope in the hearts of thousands of disabled people. On a recent radio broadcast, Joni observed, "God not only *uses* our affliction. He *designed* it." Who knows how many souls have been subject to the influence of the gospel as they model Joni's enthusiastic pattern for living? God's plans for her were for good and not for evil (see Jeremiah 29:11-13). Broken bones; broken dreams; broken hearts; put to use as only God could have planned to further the Kingdom.

Tudy is a vivacious, stalwart woman who has the gift of evangelism. She is consistent in leading souls to the Lord. People notice her wherever she goes, partly because she walks with a somewhat halted gait, the result of thirty-five surgeries during which most of her joints have been replaced: some two or three times. Friends jokingly chide her, saying that she is not crippled, just crooked. An MK (missionary kid) and part of the New Tribes family in Bolivia, eighteen-year-old Tudy was stricken with rheumatoid arthritis just as she returned to the United States for college. But it is her radiant smile and positive approach to life which intrigues others, providing unique opportunities to share her faith. As a result, many souls have been ushered into the Kingdom. She lives a normal life, and is even able to swim with the aid of a lifebelt. She freely admits that if she had not been stricken, she probably would have followed worldly pursuits. Broken to be bread for others.

Helen Keller, at nineteen months of age, was stricken with a rare infection that caused her to lose her sight and her hearing. She might have become bitter and sullen since this was the result of a doctor's error. The road she traveled was long and arduous, but she blazed new trails in living with disabilities. Helen said, "I thank God for my handicaps, for – through them – I have found myself, my work, and my God."

Emotional or physical pain is always an uninvited, unwelcome guest. It can, however, work *for* us. Through it we will probably develop compassion for others who are hurting because we know the feeling. It sharpens our focus if we remember that God has a purpose in it all, that our faith is being tested, and that He is working it together for our good (Romans 8:28). Hard times remind us that when our hearts are breaking, our witness is actually being fortified. That is when we memorized Scripture to keep focused, which inevitably leads to a closer walk with God.

Psalm 42:5 needs to become part of us. "Why are you cast down, O my soul? And why are you disquieted within me? Hope in God, for I shall yet praise Him for the help of His countenance."

Claim as your personal promises Psalm 103:13; "As a father pities his children, so the Lord pities those who fear Him."

Memorize Psalm 34:18 so that you have this truth always available to stand on when you are hurting. "The Lord is near to those who have a broken heart, and saves such as have a contrite spirit."

Called

"For the promise is unto you and to your children, and to all who are far off, as many as the Lord our God will call."

(Acts 2:39)

Countless men and women have testified to God's "call" on their lives: Florence Nightingale, Mother Teresa, and Amy Carmichael, to mention a few. J. Hudson Taylor, missionary to China during both the eighteenth and early nineteenth centuries, felt called to serve God (and he knew where), as a result of reading a tract with a Bible verse: "Who Himself bore our sins in His own body on the tree" (1 Peter 2:24). Bored, a youth of seventeen, whiling away his lunch hour (he worked for his father, a druggist); he picked up a tract which was to govern the course of his life. Dr. Martyn Lloyd-Jones, one of England's most powerful twentieth century preachers, responded to what he termed "the highest and most glorious calling to which anyone can be called," that of preaching the

Gospel. Working together with G. Campbell Morgan, these men are credited with a great revival in England. They are still respected and valued as some of the world's greatest theologians.

One pastor was saved while he was in college working towards a Ph.D. in Physiology. Almost immediately, he sensed that God was summoning him to exchange his teacher's chalk for a shepherd's staff. Although it was several years before he yielded, the call on his life was unequivocal. Ultimately, Dr. Doug responded to the "when" and "where" of God's directive and became a minister of the Gospel. Twenty years and many changed lives later, he is much loved by those who will enter Heaven's portals because a Professor of Physiology heeded God's calling.

"But what about us?" we may question. "How can we be sure of God's "call"? Perhaps, we have not had those inner promptings that others acknowledge. If so, it should boost our confidence to realize that God, through the apostle Peter, has designated five callings for each of His children.

First, we were "called out of darkness into his marvelous light" (1 Peter 2:9). This is so that we might become part of that royal priesthood that Jesus founded for us when He died on the cross for your sins and mine. We are 'called' unto Him Who is the light of the world (John 8:12). Called to be saved.

Secondly, we are called to be holy. "But as He who has 'called' you is holy, you also be holy (set apart from the world) in all your conduct" (1 Peter 1:15). We are admonished not to "conform to former lusts" (1 Peter 1:14), to be "in" the world but not "of" the world. This becomes the measure for keeping ourselves untarnished by the world system. Called to be holy.

Thirdly, we are called to take it patiently when we do well, and suffer for it. "For what credit is it if, when you are beaten for your faults, you take it patiently? But when you do good and suffer, if you take it patiently this is commendable before God. For to this you were 'called', because Christ also suffered for us, leaving us an example, that you should follow His steps" (1 Peter 2:20-21). This charge may be the most demanding of all. It may stretch us beyond pure human endurance. Each time we allow God to defend us, however, we take another step on the path to maturity. Talk with that disciple who has been in the crucible of suffering through no fault of his own, yet has purposed in his heart to love God. He radiates joy, the one who has answered the call to imitate, emulate and follow our Lord and Savior. Called to suffer.

The fourth call is found in 1 Peter 3:9. As a reward for over-coming evil and good, we are called to *inherit* a blessing. "Not returning evil for evil, or reviling for reviling, but on the contrary blessing; knowing that you were 'called,' to this, that you may inherit a blessing." Called to be and inherit a blessing.

Fifthly, in culmination of our earthly life, the call to eternal glory. "But may the God of all grace, who 'called' us to His *eternal* glory by Christ Jesus, after you have suffered a while, perfect, establish, strengthen, and settle you." (1 Peter 5:10). Called to glory.

We rejoice that we have been "called," 1-out of darkness into light; 2-to live a holy life; 3-to be willing to suffer for Christ's sake; 4-"called" to return good for evil; to be and inherit a blessing; and 5-to enter into eternal glory, where we are finally home.

"Walk worthy of the calling with which you are *called*."

(Ephesians 4:1)

Canopy of Grace

❖

"And He said to me, 'My grace is sufficient for you, for My strength is made perfect in weakness.' Therefore most gladly I will rather boast in my infirmities, that the power of Christ may *rest* upon me." (2 Corinthians 12:9)

What began as an ordinary Sunday morning—breakfast with an eye on the clock, not wanting to be late for Sunday School and church—developed into a most <u>extra</u>-ordinary day. As I poured a bowl of cereal, I became painfully aware of a series of violent, pulsating convulsions in my left leg. I tipped slightly over to one side, realizing that I had lost control over part of my body. Hobbling toward the bed-room, my mind began to spin. This was unlike anything I had experienced before. I figured it was, in all likelihood, a TIA, (Transient Ischemic Attack)or in layman's terms, a mini-stroke. I lay quietly on my bed for ten to fifteen minutes allowing my mind and body to settle down.

As I sensed that whatever was happening was beyond my control, an incredible calm descended upon me. Some how I knew this crisis was an encounter with God. I spoke audibly to Him saying, "Lord, I know that You will cause this to work together for my good, according to Romans 8:28 – I don't see how, but You promised. Thank you." The rest is history. I summoned help and wound up in the hospital. Praise God for His timely sense of humor.

The emergency room physician asked, "Did you lose the capacity to speak?"

"No, I kept talking," I replied.

"Who did you talk to?" the nice doctor asked.

"God," I ventured and then, when his pen stopped in mid-air, I added sheepishly, "and myself," so they wouldn't wheel me off to the psychiatric ward.

But the fact remains I *had* communed with the Lord. Following several months of rest, therapy, and most importantly the faithful prayers of many dear saints, I recovered. During recuperation, 2 Corinthians 12:9, as given to us by the Apostle Paul, literally became a part of my being as God revealed Himself to me more clearly then I had ever experienced before.

When I learned that the word "rest" in 2 Corinthians 12:9 appears only this one time in Scripture, it captured my attention. It is from the Greek word "episkenoo" which means to tabernacle over; pitch a tent over; dwell upon. Thus Christ's power literally covers us—"rests" upon us as did the cloud and the pillar of fire over the Israelites during their wilderness journey. When we have no power of our own; when we are at our weakest point; when we need it most; the Lord "tabernacles" over us, His power resting on us. We need not strive to attain this rest; we really cannot accomplish it of ourselves; we are helpless to attain such a level of rest. We merely need to; "Be still and know that I am God" (Psalm 46:10). During moments of crisis, our loving Father mercifully protects us with a covering—His canopy of grace.

Thank you, Abba Father, for the assurance that whatever the future holds, truly Your grace *is* sufficient for Your children.

Changed

"But we all, with unveiled face beholding as in a mirror the glory of the Lord, are transformed into the same image from glory to glory, just as by the Spirit of the Lord."

(2 Corinthians 3:l8)

From struggle to struggle: Do you remember what problems you were wrestling with a year ago? Perhaps they have been resolved, perhaps not. Either way, if you did not allow bitterness to take over but sought God's direction through His Word, prayer, and Godly counsel, you have become a better reflection of the Lord than you were before your struggle.

From strength to strength: To whom do you turn when you think you have reached the end of your rope? We have a choice. We can throw up our hands, feeling that we just can't handle our situation, or "come boldly to the throne of grace, that we may obtain mercy and find grace to help, in time of need" (Hebrews 4:16). God has promised us sufficient grace. He offers us His strength in exchange for our weakness (see 2 Corinthians 12:9). That's a bargain! Operating in His strength is bound to lead us to victory.

From experience to experience: Are you a victim of circumstances over which you have no control? Most of us are at one time or another. But we do control our responses. An old adage states: "It's not the force of the gale, but the set of the sail, that determines the course of life." Strong ships were not made for safe harbor. Charles Swindoll in his discourse on "Attitude" says, "I am convinced that life is 10% what happens to me and 90% how I react to it."

From glory to glory: As we attempt to keep our focus on God in the tough times, He promises that He will "transform" us into His own image from glory to glory by the Spirit of the Lord (see 2 Corinthians 3:18). Just as the caterpillar becomes a butterfly, we too will be changed to be more like Him. Experts in the field of psychology claim that we become more like the people whom we think about most—for better or worse. We can strive to be more like Jesus, but it is only as we continue to "behold (in the Word of God) as in a mirror, the glory of the

Lord" (see 2 Corinthians 3:18) and fixing our eyes on Jesus that we will reflect His glory and be changed.

Christian Trees

"And out of the ground God made every tree grow that is pleasant to the sight and good for food. The tree of life was also in the midst of the garden, and the tree of the knowledge of good and evil." (Genesis 2:9 NAS)

C hristmas, the celebration of the birth of God's only begotten son, Jesus Christ, probably brings into play more traditions—both Biblical and secular—than any other date on our calendar. One of the most prevalent of these customs is the Christmas tree which takes up residence in many homes in Christendom. Martin Luther is credited with bringing the evergreen into his home and lighting it with candles, symbolizing Christ as the Light of the world. Thus, the tradition of decorating trees with lights and ornaments was born. Some people feel that we have carried it too far, tending to worship the symbolic tree rather than Jesus Christ Himself.

The Scriptures refer more often to trees (about 550 times) than to any other living thing except people. There are at least 26 different varieties mentioned. We find repeated allegorical references to men and trees, all in a *favorable* light. The average tree absorbs carbon dioxide at a rate of 48 pounds per year and releases enough oxygen back into the atmosphere to support two human beings. One of the most fascinating facts is that when a tree is in distress, it sends out signals. These signals attract enemies such as insects and disease, making the tree vulnerable. However, as soon as a tree signals distress, the closest tree will return those signals, by way of signifying support. It encourages the distressed tree to "hang in there and not give up," according to a Conservation Workshop (Joan Clayton.) God planned for mankind and trees to support one another, as part of the balance of nature.

Biblically, there are **four trees** that make the difference between life and death. Genesis 2:9 tells us that in the Garden of Eden, the original garden of creation, God placed the **"tree of life"** (#1) and the **"tree of the knowledge of good and evil"** (#2) (Genesis 2:9). He then put man into the garden to "tend" (guard, protect, preserve, have charge of) it. God said that Adam and Eve should not eat of the second tree, under penalty of death. We know that they disobeyed God; succumbed to the serpent's temptation; and ate forbidden fruit, which resulted in their knowledge of good and evil. So

God barred them from the paradise garden of Eden where they might have lived forever. The second tree thus became symbolic of the fall of man, a tree of death.

The **third tree** is the one on which the history of man hinges; a tree which was formed into a cross and placed on a hill called Calvary. God sent His only begotten Son here to earth so that His entire creation might be reconciled to Him. This tree bore Jesus Christ, who was sacrificed; bearing the full weight of every sin from Adam and Eve's to yours and mine. Jesus willingly paid the penalty—dying on this tree so that we might be forgiven and reconciled to God. He was taken down from the cross, buried, and rose again the third day, heralding the defeat of death and proclaiming victory for all who place their trust in Him (see1 Corinthians 15:3-4). Tree #3 is the one on which we focus—"that old rugged cross, the emblem of suffering and shame," where Christ purchased our redemption with His precious blood (see 1 Peter 1:18-19).

Tree #4 is that which is depicted by the Apostle John in Revelation 2:7, "To him who overcomes I will give to eat from the tree of life, which is in the midst of the Paradise of God." We have come full circle: the tree of life at the time of creation to the tree of death to the tree of atonement to the tree of life in the New Jerusalem. The first and last reference to a specific tree in the Bible is to this "tree of life."

In the final chapter of the Bible (Revelation 22:1-3), we are told, "on either side of the river is the tree of life, which bears twelve fruits, each tree yielding its fruit every month. The leaves of the tree are for the healing of the nations. And there shall be no more curse." Man's access to the first tree of life was denied because of sin but in the restored Heavenly Paradise, every believer will eat of this "tree of life" and will live forever (see Revelation 22).We celebrate the birth of the Babe in the Manger born in Bethlehem two centuries ago. We must remember that the Babe left the manger and went to the cross to pay the wages of sin. Christmas trees or Christian trees, it is the worth of Jesus Christ which commands our worship and to whom we offer it.

"Joy to the world, the Lord is come. Let earth receive her King."

Cleansed

"You are already clean because of the Word, which I have spoken to you." (John 15:3)

My quiet time that morning lacked luster. Although I was reluctant to admit it, problems with broken marriages, single parent heartaches, wayward grandchildren and poor health clouded my mind to the point where I was unable to concentrate on the words before me. Have you ever experienced a "desert" period like that? According to Exodus, Chapter 3, Moses tended his father-in-law's sheep on the "backside of the desert" for forty years (earning his "BD": degree, as some wag expressed it); then God spoke to him. Since I was in the "middle of a muddle"—my singular desert place—God's call to Moses from the burning bush seemed pretty remote. I was certainly not hearing anything! It was April, one of the hottest months of the year in the South of India, (Andhra Pradesh), where I had been living for the past few weeks with friends.

My host, C.D. Benjamin, was a third generation Christian, his grandfather having been a Brahman priest who had been converted to Christianity by a rickshaw driver on the road many years previously. "C.D." was a respected Bible teacher whom God had used to plant more than twenty-five indigenous Christian churches in South India.

At dinner, that evening, I confessed to him, "I am discouraged because in reading the Word of God lately, I am not assimilating it. My mind is like a sieve."

My mentor/friend calmly replied, "Sister, when you take a sieve and pour water over and over through it, one thing is certain. That sieve is clean!"

What a simple truth. Uncomplicated! My spirit fairly soared. I began to embrace what God was teaching me.

"Christ also loved the church and gave Himself for her, that He might sanctify and <u>cleanse</u> her with the washing of water by the word" (Ephesians 5:25-26). No more fussing—there is no such thing as reading God's Word in vain. We can relax. The Holy Spirit cleanses our minds, as we delve into His Word, while the blood of Jesus Christ cleanses our hearts.

"God will not allow His Word to return unto Him void, but will accomplish what He pleases and it will prosper in the thing for which He sent it." (Isaiah 55:11)

Clouds

"He makes the clouds His chariot; He walks upon the wings of the wind." (Psalm 104:3)

A perennial topic—the weather; hot or cold; rain or shine. It's what everybody talks about, but aside from prognosticating, nobody does anything about it—except God. Scientists have developed methods of altering local patterns, but God alone is empowered to use it as He wills. He stills the storm; He calms the sea and He makes the clouds His chariot.

Do you ever feel literally weighted down, at an impasse, where you seem to be laboring beneath a heaviness best described as an oppressive, dark cloud? Would it help to be assured that there is an element of truth in the old saying, "Every cloud has a silver lining"? God's Word gives us cause to believe it.

Before God gave the Ten Commandments, He said to Moses, "Behold, I am coming to you in a thick cloud, that the people may hear when I speak with you and believe you forever" (Exodus I9:9). Not only does God come to us in or on the clouds, but He uses these same vehicles to speak to us—often loud and clear.

Consider these passages from the Old Testament: "Then Moses went up into the mountain, and a cloud covered the mountain. Now the glory of the Lord rested on Mount Sinai, and the cloud covered it six days. And on the seventh day the Lord called to Moses 'out of the midst' of the cloud." (Exodus 24:15-16) "Now the Lord descended 'in the cloud', and stood there with him (Moses) and proclaimed the name of the Lord..." (Exodus 34:5). "Then the Lord came down 'in the cloud,' and spoke to him (Moses), and took of the Spirit that was upon him, and placed the same Spirit upon the seventy elders" (Numbers 11:25).

In each of these instances, God's message radically changed Moses' life—either offering relief from dire circumstances or confirming His compassion, loving-kindness and mercy. In like manner, during those times in our lives when we cannot see the sun through the clouds, it follows that if we trust God and give heed to His voice, He will grant to us comfort and relief. He may offer a change of direction or encourage us to hang in there a little longer. He may be wooing us to promote a closer walk. Whatever our distress—our cloud, we can expect Him to impart something very personal and very special. He has not changed. He may speak by His Spirit through the Word, a godly friend, prayer, or a drastic change, but without a doubt, He *will* speak. There is no need to feel threatened when a cloud appears on our horizon. God may come to us in the clouds as a still, small voice.

Let our prayer be, "God, cause us to hearken for your voice, knowing that You are there." Let us remember that a tear in the eye produces a rainbow in the heart. Cause us to look for that bow of promise knowing that You see the whole world from Your chariot of clouds.

God spoke to Peter, James and John from a cloud on the Mount of Transfiguration, announcing: "This is my beloved Son, in whom I am well pleased. Hear ye Him" (Matthew 17:5 KJV). So it was from a cloud that Christ's identity was first revealed to the disciples at the beginning of His ministry. And it is from the clouds that Jesus will come at last, "Then we who are alive and remain shall be caught up together with them in the clouds, to meet the Lord in the air; and so shall we ever be with the Lord. Therefore comfort one another with these words" (1 Thessalonians 4:17-18).

"At that time they will see the Son of Man coming in a cloud with power and great glory." (Luke 21:27)

Communication

"A word fitly spoken is like apples of gold in settings of silver." (Proverbs 25:11)

Communication—we live in an age where there is more exchange of information than at any other time in recorded history. Our world has become smaller and smaller. We have easy access to data reaching back thousands of years. In addition, we have radio, television, computers, newspapers and periodicals that publish events as soon as they occur, keeping us well informed. Whereas the media may be biased and sometimes inaccurate, people are privy to current developments from all parts of the known world. Thus, we are affected emotionally by events in Iraq or Israel almost as soon as they happen. We make personal contacts with one another almost instantly via the telephone or e-mail. Corresponding by letter ("snail mail") is fast becoming a lost art, in the interest of time. But the woeful truth is that all of this rapid-fire delivery is proving to be detrimental to inter-personal, "one-on-one" relationships. We can easily suppress our true feelings which lead to restrained, almost superficial communication.

Nothing takes the place of spending time with family and those who are dear to us, as we engage in purposeful heart-to-heart conversations. However, long distances and tight schedules prevent us from gathering together as much as we would like. Years may go by until suddenly we are faced with a crisis and struck with the realization that we have never shared our innermost feelings with or about those we love. This is especially true when we are faced with a terminal illness, either ours or a family member or a friend.

Sue, a trainer of hospice personnel, recommends using an approach written by Dr. Ira Byock, a physician who has dealt primarily with end-of-life issues. This model has been incor-porated into a hospice program, for families of the terminally ill with great success. However, it is equally effective where any breach of communication has occurred; where there is a wounded or broken relationship; or where you would just like to make a good relationship better.

The five key areas are:

1. I love you. (Explore as fully as you comfortably can the reasons why.)

2. I forgive you. (For not understanding me when...or for being angry, etc.)
3. Do you forgive me? (For totaling the car when I was 16, for disobeying)
4. Thank you. (For being there when I needed you, for being my friend)
5. Goodbye. (I will miss you but I will be okay. It's alright for you to go...)

This is merely an example. Each person must follow his or her own heart, based on their history with the recipient, and each step should be bathed in prayer.

As you think about your own relationship, you might have determined not to wait for a final communication; rather you may wish to bless someone you care for, a son or a daughter-in-law or another family member. A correspondence beginning with "I love you" and based on this method of dealing with issues, past and present, could serve to nourish your hearts and knit them together as never before. A daughter recently wrote such a letter to her Mom, delineating some of her finer attributes as reasons for "I love you." She offered forgiveness to her Mother for not understanding her feelings about certain things when she was younger; asking forgiveness for causing any unnecessary worry. She thanked her Mom for being a role model in several areas of life; and ended with a prayer that "left nothing unsaid and that there would be no regrets about our relationship when we leave planet earth." Her Mother insists that the letter was so edifying that she has been floating on a cloud of sublimity ever since receiving it. I should know. I am that Mother.

It is easier for many of us to convey our feelings by letter than to verbalize them. Words, written or audible, have power to soothe and to heal so don't procrastinate. Communicate God's love.

"A man has joy by the answer of his mouth; and a word spoken in due season, how good it is!" (Proverbs 15:23)

Cottonwood Tree

"But his delight is in the law of the Lord; and in his law he meditates day and night. He shall be like a tree planted by the rivers of water, that brings forth his fruit in its season; whose leaf also shall not wither; and whatever he does shall prosper." (Psalm I:2-3)

A longside the path in our back lot, a twenty-foot limb from a large cottonwood tree lay sprawled on the ground, victim of a spring windstorm. Grateful that no damage had occurred when it fell, I made a mental note to have it removed; then promptly stored the idea away in my "forgettery." Several months later, I noticed that the neglected limb had produced numerous buds. Some of the buds were on branches up to six feet long, although it lay there devoid of nourishment—sustained only by the remaining life within. In due time, those buds unfolded, disclosing an array of glossy, green leaves. They waved a breezy "hello" in a rather proud display.

Friends admired their beauty and commented that it was quite a feat that these branches were thriving apart from the tree. We speculated how long this would go on. Alas! The saga ended after one or two weeks. Foliage which a few days ago, spoke life and beauty, was now crackled, withered and quite dead. Meanwhile, leaves on the mother tree flourish as they complete their annual cycle.

The lesson is clear. Unless we partake regularly of the living Word, we leave ourselves open to spiritual decay. It may be a well kept secret when, for a few days, our schedules do not "allow" time for Bible reading, study or communion with God. However, if the trend continues our families and close friends are sure to notice. We will no longer be able to provide the encouragement and support they need, because our spiritual reserve is depleted. When this becomes a pattern, in due time, everybody will know. Our visage will change. We will no longer have the capacity to bear fruit.

Unlike the cottonwood limb, however, we can reverse the process simply by being in the Word faithfully, daily. When Paderwski, the great concert pianist, spoke about his routine, he confirmed the need for daily practice. He said that if he missed a day, he would notice a difference in his playing. If he missed several days, the critics would notice the difference. If he did not practice for a week, the public would notice the difference.

"Abide in me, and I in you; as the branch cannot bear fruit of itself, unless it abides in the vine; neither can you, unless you abide in Me." (John l5:4)

David's Five Smooth Stones

❖

"He (David) chose for himself five smooth stones from the brook and put them in a shepherd's bag, in a pouch which he had, and his sling was at his hand. And he drew near to the Philistine." (1 Samuel 17:40)

Ask any child in a Sunday School class to recount one or two of his favorite Bible Stories and you will find that the story of David and Goliath ranks high on the list. We all take great delight in the victory that a mere teenager won as he slew Goliath the Philistine giant, and delivered God's people, the Israelites

Confident that the battle was the Lord's and that He would give the enemy into Israel's hands, David "chose for himself five smooth stones from a brook." He killed the giant with only one shot from his sling. Why did he select five stones? We really don't know. Some have suggested that it was symbolic because Goliath had four remaining brothers—all giants of

Gath, who would one day be slain by David's men, as recounted in the book of 1 Chronicles 20:4-8. This is strictly conjecture, of course. But it is significant that they were smooth stones which, when airborne from a sling, would find their mark much more readily than a rough-edged, jagged piece of rock.

"Five smooth stones chosen from a brook." David knew where to look. The brook would yield smooth stones. Today, so-called "rock hounds" collect semi-precious and precious stones and "tumble" them in a machine containing water and various types of grit to break off any uneven, unsightly edges before shaping and designing them to be worn as jewelry. This is the art of "Lapidary." Testing is done to determine the amount of pressure and vibration to be applied to each "batch" of stones, the proper level of stress to be exerted, and length of time required to produce the desired texture without fracturing the gems. Using a continual water wash, this tumbling process yields beautiful, polished gems. Those pretty, smooth stones that we find along the seashore were created by God, the first "Lapidary," using the ocean as the original tumbler. It rolls stone over stone, using sand as an abrasive to smooth and shape each one.

God refers to us in 1 Peter 2:5-6 as being like "living stones, being built up into a spiritual house…to offer up spiritual sacrifices acceptable to God through Jesus Christ" who is the Chief Cornerstone. How does He smooth and shape us?

Are we dealing with an "irregular" person or faced with harsh circumstances? Perhaps we can more readily embrace our trial if we realize that we have been chosen as "living stones" and may need a bit of "tumbling" as part of "being built up into a spiritual house." Our offering, our spiritual sacrifice is a life pleasing to Him. So when the grit is chipping away at our flaws, the friction becomes painful, and all about us is topsy-turvy in the heat of our singular kiln, isn't it comforting to know that the Master Lapidary is actually tumbling us with a particular end in view?

Once the water of the Word has washed the grit asunder and we have endured just the right amount of abrasion, we will find that just as David's smooth stone was aimed perfectly at the giant, so God will point us in the right direction, empowering us to hit the mark and to slay our Goliaths.

"For it is God who works in you both to will and to do for His good pleasure." (Philippians 2:13)

Day of Small Things

❖

"For who has despised the day of small things?"

(Zechariah 4:10)

The question was directed by the minor prophet, Zechariah, to the Jews who had returned to Jerusalem from Babylonian captivity, around 400 B.C., but it applied to all of God's people. It still does. It was asked in derision. His objective was to put to rest the mockery and scoffing that was being hurled at a small remnant of souls who were working hard to rebuild the temple. Those dissenters, who did not believe that there were sufficient resources or enough people with the tenacity and skills to complete it, had not reckoned with the fact that "little is much when God is in it." They despised the *day of small things.* Do we? God does not.

The Lord anointed David, youngest and smallest of Jesse's eight sons, to be king over Israel (see 1 Samuel 16). Gideon, a farmer, was professedly the "least and weakest in his father's house." In a ludicrous (from man's point of view) display of power, using pitchers, torches and trumpets, according to God's plan, Gideon and a small army of 300 men defeated the Midianites who had ruled over Israel for seven years, leaving them bereft of crops and livestock. Gideon, an ordinary man, won an extra-ordinary battle over Israel's enemy for the glory of God (see Judges 7).

At one time during Jesus' earthly ministry, on a mountain near the Sea of Galilee, He fed at least 5,000 men besides women and children with just five loaves and two fish which a small boy had brought with him. After they all had eaten, there were twelve full baskets remaining (see John 6:1-15). Here, at possibly the most famous picnic of all time, Jesus used the meager offering of a child to perform a miracle. Later, He fed 4,000 people with but seven loaves of bread and a few fish, having seven baskets or hampers full left over (see Mark 8: 18-21). Little becomes much when God is in it. Later, a certain widow put all she had—two mites (lepta), probably the small-est coin of its time—in the treasury. The rich gave large sums but her scant, sacrificial gift has been set forth as a virtuous example for generations to follow (see Mark 12:41-44). Don't despise the small things.

The Apostle Peter was imprisoned during King Herod's rampage against the early Christian church. One night an angel appeared, awaking him and telling him to "gird yourself and tie on your sandals" (Acts 12:8) He did. Then the angel and Peter walked right through the iron gate which opened of its own accord, spelling freedom. When we can't see a way out of our "prison," in the words of Bible teacher C.D. Benjamin of India, "Don't you think that a God who cares about Peter's shoes is conscious of your needs also?" Don't despise the small things.

Brother Lawrence, a seventeenth century monk, is best known for his little book, *"Practicing the Presence of God,"* which has motivated millions of readers to yearn for more intimacy with God. He is often referred to as the "pots and pans" monk because he was assigned to kitchen detail much of the time. Of course, his life in the monastery involved the priestly prayers and meditations that comprise the life of a monk. But when he was inspired to journal what he counted some of his most precious moments, he wrote, "We can do *little things* for God. I turn the cake that is frying." He realized that we can take joy in performing ordinary, mundane tasks if we do them as unto the Lord, and that God is especially pleased when we sense His presence as we perform those daily chores.

The diary of a preacher, discovered after he died, read: "Spent the day fishing with my boy. Nothing much accomplished today." His son went on to become a great man of God and he pointed to that special day with his Dad as the day when he gave himself to God. He wanted to be like his father, who "worked for God" and still took time to go fishing with his son. Knowing that God is glorified in what "appears" to be insignificant should encourage us to offer up for His blessing such simple things as planting a garden; folding laundry; preparing dinner for a neighbor who is ill; or sitting with a sick child. Like Brother Lawrence, we may "turn the cake that is frying" and thank God for the "day of small things."

Queen Victoria of England was led to Jesus Christ through her governess, who was saved through John Wesley. She maintained that she was saved by an "m" in the Bible. "For you see your calling, brethren, that not many wise according to the flesh, not many mighty, not many noble, are called" (1 Corinthians 1:26). Without the "m"- if God had said "not any noble" - all nobility would have been excluded from God's family. She thanked God for the "m" in her Bible, a small thing.

"For whosoever shall give you a cup of water to drink in my name, because you belong to Christ…he shall not lose his reward." (Mark 9:41)

Deliverance or Disaster

"And the Angel of God, who went before the camp of Israel, moved and went behind them; and the pillar of cloud went from before them and stood behind them." (Exodus 14:19)

We should never cease to be amazed at the ingenuity with which God defeats the enemy and saves His people, using the very same tool to do both at the same time. One such illustration is found in Exodus 14:20 with regard to a cloud. "So it (the cloud) came between the camp of the Egyptians and the camp of Israel." Thus, it was a cloud and darkness to the one, and it gave light by night to the other, so that the enemy did not come near the Israelites all that night. Notice how that which provided light for God's children spelled darkness and disaster to their enemies.

After the night had passed, God repeated the process, this time using the Red Sea in a display of power. As the Egyptian chariots pursued the Israelites, He divided the waters, allowing

His children to cross over safely to the opposite shore. "The Lord caused the sea to go back by a strong east wind all that night, and made the sea into dry land, and the waters were divided" (Exodus 14:21). The next morning as the Egyptians tried to overtake the Israelites, the Lord commanded Moses to stretch out his hand over the sea and it returned to its normal level, rendering the chariot wheels useless, and drowning— annihilating—the Egyptian horde, so that the Israelites' escape was ensured and once again, salvation for His own and death for the scoffers.

God's hand was upon Moses from the time his mother, Jochebed, gave him birth. Pharaoh had ordered that every Hebrew baby boy should be cast into the Nile River because the Israelites were growing in strength and number; becoming a threat to Egypt (see Genesis 2:22). After his mother had hidden him for three months, she made an ark of bulrushes, put the child in it and laid it in the reeds by the river's bank. Pharaoh's daughter rescued and adopted Moses, who became a prince of the royal family. He left Egypt at age forty and returned at age eighty to deliver his people from their tormentors. The Nile River, which the enemy had designated for Hebrew infanticide, was the very instrument which God used to protect Moses, who would later destroy the Egyptians and deliver the Israelites.

Years before, when people had become so wicked that they provoked God's wrath, He gave a man named Noah instructions to build a boat (the ark) that would become the means of carrying him and his family to safety. "Noah found grace in the eyes of the Lord" (Genesis 6:8). Water covered the earth (the great flood) destroying the people and the evil they were perpetrating in their hearts, but a remnant was saved. The same vehicle (the waters) that destroyed those of a reprobate heart floated the ark and became the means whereby God's people were brought to safety.

The ultimate act of Providence was realized when God gave His only begotten Son to die an ignominious death on the Cross of Calvary. Here Jesus Christ took all our sins—yours and mine—upon Himself. But the Power of His Resurrection spoke deliverance to His children and disaster to the enemy of their souls.

In the Apostle Paul's time, when a Roman general or emperor won a battle, he would come home and parade down the Via Sacra (the main road), followed by carriers of great torches of incense, proclaiming victory. But the unfortunate captives were dragged along behind them, chained to the chariots. The incense literally smelled of victory to the army and defeat to its captives. Symbolically, now more than 2,000 years later, God commissions His children, as trophies of

Christ's victory, to go out into the world to spread the fragrance of the knowledge of God everywhere.

According to the 2nd Chapter of 2nd Corinthians, we are "the fragrance of Christ among those who are being saved and among those who are perishing." To the one we are the aroma (fragrance) of life unto life—vital, healthy, living; and to the other the aroma (a fatal odor) of death unto death. The Word of God spells deliverance for His people, and disaster to the mocker. Which fragrance do you prefer?

"He who believes in Him is not condemned, but he who does not believe is condemned already, because he has not believed in the name of the only begotten Son of God."

(John 3:18)

Does Your Anchor Hold?

❖

"This hope we have as an anchor of the soul, both sure and steadfast." (Hebrews 6:19)

We were studying the above passage from the book of Hebrews with a small group of friends when Bob, premier sailor and skipper, recalled the unusual manner in which his yacht had once won a special race. A strong current had deterred the "fleet" but there was just enough breeze to fill the sails, creating the illusion that they were all making slow progress. Actually, they were drifting backward at a rate so slow that the crews were unaware of their plight. Sensing what was happening, the skipper instructed his crew to drop anchor discreetly on the leeward side enabling his vessel to hold fast. Guess who won the race?

A convocation or solemn assembly of mostly believers from South East India was conducted at one of our state universities, as in Joel 1:14. Brother Bakht Singh, a converted

Sikh, brought a stirring message wherein he likened the basic Christian principles in Acts 2:42 to anchors in our lives. Immediately following the birth of the New Testament Church at Pentecost, three thousand souls were saved. Discipling newborn babes in Christ is expedient, especially where there is an evangelism explosion such as this. We are told that they "continued steadfastly in the apostles' doctrine and fellowship, in the breaking of bread, and in prayers." These four anchors prevented them from drifting aimlessly, needlessly toward dangerous reefs and shoals.

Anchor One Speaks of Doctrine: Doctrine based on sound Biblical principles rather than the traditions of men or their varied experiences is vital to a steadfast walk with God. Titus 1:9 states that an elder must "holding fast the faithful *word* as he has been taught, that he may be able, by sound *doctrine*, both to exhort and convict those who contradict."

Anchor Two Speaks of Fellowship: Fellowship or communion, from the Greek "koinonia," is sharing our blessings and encouraging us to risk loving others, even as we are loved. Jesus told us to, "Love one another as I have loved you" (John 13:34).

Anchor Three Speaks of the Lord's Supper: It calls us to accountability and self-examination. 1 Corinthians 10:21 warns us that we "cannot partake of the cup of the Lord and the cup of demons." There is strength and stability in remembering our Lord through the broken bread and the cup. These ideals or standards of conduct, virtuous as they may be, would be lost on us, however, without the fourth anchor.

Anchor Four Speaks of Prayer: We need to be in consistent communication with our Lord through prayer. Prayer is the key that unlocks the door to the heart of God. "Pray without ceasing" (I Thessalonians 5:l7).

By the time the competition in the yacht race discovered their backward drift, it was too late. Failing to lay anchor, they were unable to overcome the lead that had been established, thereby losing the race. Spurgeon said: "The Bible is a harbor where I can drop down my anchor; feeling certain that it will hold. Here is a place where I can find sure footing, and, by the grace of God, from this confidence I shall never be moved."

Let's make sure that our anchors hold us both sure and steadfast, like the Apostle Paul: "Then fearing lest we should run aground on the rocks, they dropped four anchors from the stern, and prayed for day to come" (Acts 27:29).

Doors of Circumstance

"And to the angel of the church in Philadelphia write: These things says he who is holy, he who is true, he who has the key of David, he who opens, and no one shuts; and shuts and no one opens." (Revelation 3:7-8)

As always, God's message is a timely one for you and me. Most of us have waited tentatively for God to open a door to our hopes and dreams. You may have submitted an application for college, or applied for a loan in anticipation of a new car or that dream home. Are you anxiously awaiting the results of a job interview? Does it seem as if your future is only as predictable as an unpredictable corporation executive? Or maybe you are in the arena of suffering and have fought until you are exhausted. Keep in mind that the God of providence, the God of circumstance, holds the Master Key to your life and mine.

In the Book of Second Kings, God has chronicled accounts of healed hurts and hearts for our edification. Second Kings Chapter 4 tells of a "certain" woman who appeals to the prophet, Elisha, for help. (Though we are ordinary people, God knows us individually as "certain" men and women, worthy of His attention and honorable mention.) All we know of the lady's background is that her husband has died and she is poverty-stricken. She is in danger of losing her two sons to creditors in accordance with the custom and laws of that day. This certain woman has come up against a closed door, with no way out. But God is about to deal with a common situation in a most uncommon way. Elisha learns that she has nothing in the house but a jar of oil. He sends her to the neighbors to borrow empty vessels. When this is done, he tells her to "shut the door" behind her and her sons; then "fill all the empty vessels and set them aside" (Second Kings 4:3-4).

She may consider the idea preposterous, but she does it anyway. God's way. This closed door is a golden opportunity upon which "hinges" the provision for all her needs. Closed doors are not always bad news. 2 Kings 4:5 says, the widow "went from him and shut the door behind her" (a door of obedience). Then when the vessels are all filled, the man of God tells her to go sell the oil, pay her debts, and live on the rest providing for all her needs.

Later on, Elisha meets a prominent Shunammite woman who urges her husband to make a place for him to stay, a prophet's chamber, whenever he is in the area (see 2 Kings 4:8-10). "Do not forget to entertain strangers, for by so doing some have unwittingly entertained angels" (Hebrews 13:2). In return for her hospitality, Elisha desired to bless this lady. When he calls for her, she comes and "stands in the doorway," never dreaming that this was her doorway to hope. But it is. He promises that, even though her husband is old, she shall bear a son within the year, which she does (see 2 Kings 4:15-17). The lad grows until one day he is suddenly smitten and dies. His mother lays him on the prophet's bed, "shut(s) the door" and runs to search for the prophet, hoping that he can help her (see 2 Kings 4:19-37).

(Sadly, we are apt to shut the door of our hearts in a time of grief, closing ourselves off from God and others, unwilling to share our pain.) When they returned to the room where the dead child lay, Elisha "went in and shut the door behind the two of them and prayed to the Lord" (2 Kings 4:33). This supplication from Elisha's "secret closet" leads God to display His resurrection power. The boy is made alive!

Doors closed by God often point us to fertile paths of opportunity, provision, and blessing.

"When you have 'shut your door,' pray to your Father who is in the secret place, and your Father who sees in secret will reward you openly." (Matthew 6:6)

Eighteen Inches Too High

✤

"If thou shalt confess with thy mouth the Lord Jesus and shalt believe in thine heart that God hath raised Him from the dead, thou shalt be saved." (Romans I0:9 KJV)

The tragic story of an airliner that crashed on a Nevada mountain top in a blinding snowstorm appeared in the headlines of a major U.S. daily newspaper. All aboard were killed. The airliner was only five minutes from Las Vegas airport at the time of the crash. The article quoted a deputy sheriff at the scene of the wreckage as saying, "If that plane had been I8 inches higher, it would have cleared the mountain top!" The title of the account read, "18" Too Low!"

Our hearts grieve at the realization that those lives hinged on a brief I8 inch gap. However, an old adage states that the greatest distance in the world is the approximate I8 inches between man's head and his heart. Many dear souls have consented to God's perfect plan of salvation—mentally affirming the truth that Jesus Christ lived on earth, died on the cross for our sins, was buried, rose again the third day, ascended, and is seated at the right hand of God the Father, alive forevermore. But if the message has not seeped down into their hearts, they are lost.

Some people carry this head knowledge for many years before their hearts claim Christ as their personal Savior. Romans 10:10 states, "For with the heart man believeth unto righteousness; and with the mouth confession is made unto salvation" (KJV). Heart belief is essential to salvation. Beloved, let us make sure that we are not denied an entrance to an eternal heavenly home because of a faith that is 18 inches too high!

Every End = A New Beginning

✤

"A land for which the LORD your God cares; the eyes of the LORD your God are always on it, from the beginning of the year to the very end of the year." (Deuteronomy 11:12)

Newspaper headlines, radio, and TV, all shout out the news! The old year is ending; a New Year begins. The world is still at war; the kids have grown a year older, a bit taller and a lot sassier; those gray hairs have multiplied; those aching muscles and stiff joints are probably *not* just because you slept in the wrong position, and if we need further confirmation, our calendar changes from an "old" year to a "new" one. Let's face it, last year has *ebbed* and we are perched on the threshold of an unpredictable new one.

Wicked King Nebuchadnezzar of Babylon was warned by God (who spoke to Daniel through a dream) to "break off your sins by being righteous, and your iniquities by showing mercy to the poor." He stubbornly refused to do so. At the end of twelve months (a year), judgment fell upon him and he suffered a horrific fate. He lost his kingdom; lost his mind; lost everything (Daniel 4:27-33).

What if we only had these next twelve months in which to "shape up"? What would we do differently than we have in the past as we begin our year of *new beginnings*?

Every end is a new beginning. While it may not be earth-shaking news, it is cause for careful examination. "New beginning" sounds a bit redundant. But when we begin a new venture—plant a seed, build a house, start a business—all these things are technically "new." Conversely, there is the situation where we have tried to say "no" to a bad habit, but didn't quite make it. Smokers share a classic line: "I *have* quit smoking…several times." Now, having decided to put forth the effort once more—whatever the habit—we start over afresh; but it is not exactly "new." We merely begin again.

Bullfrogs and butterflies are patterned after this type of renewal. A tiny tadpole propelled under water by its squiggly tail, one day becomes a frog who sits when he stands and stands when he sits, and his guttural croaking amuses us all. A small caterpillar living in a hard-shelled chrysalis, sleeps on a milkweed leaf and awakens one morning, struggles a bit, then emerges from confinement to become a beautiful monarch butterfly. His wings carry him from flower to flower as he experiences renewal.

One of the most mystical of all beginnings is the birth of a newborn child. We marvel at the tiny bundle with skin as soft as down, and the wee little brow all wrinkled in a frown. The baby grows from childhood to adolescence, plunges into the teen (sometimes turbulent) years, after which he or she must make choices regarding their future. This usually necessitates leaving home, which means that parents are thrust into a *new beginning.* It has become known as the "empty nest" syndrome. Almost without warning life is different, a bit on the off-side. The house is quiet and sometimes the silence is deafening. The old has passed away. The new has come. This is a golden opportunity for parents to re-discover each other, pursue a hobby, take a mini-vacation and/or dig a little deeper into God's Word together to mine the "treasures of darkness and hidden riches of secret places" (Isaiah 45:3).

The greatest beginning of all occurs when a person dead in sin becomes born anew of the Spirit—when he or she has passed from certain death to eternal life. The Decision Magazine re-counted the story of a man who had just finished dinner at a Salvation Army Church. He was encouraged to attend the meeting. He was drunk at the time and homeless, having been a street person for twenty years. A counselor from the crusade offered to protect his shopping cart containing all his earthly possessions, (including bottles for recycling), if he would go to the crusade. Reluctantly, he went.

There he received Christ and left his old life behind. Later, he said, "I was going around in the same circle and never finding any answers. This is my 'new beginning'." Every believer in Jesus Christ has experienced this, and we have the joyful anticipation of yet another *beginning*—Heaven. Let us be on the alert and watch for every opportunity to share the Good News. Wouldn't it be great if the Holy Spirit used each one of us to lead another person into the Kingdom during the coming year? Wow! Talk about "new beginnings"!

"Therefore, if any man be in Christ he is a new creation; old things have passed away; behold, all things have become new." (2 Corinthians 5:17)

Forgive and Forget ?

❖

"Be kind to one another, tenderhearted, forgiving one another, even as God in Christ forgave you."

(Ephesians 4:32)

"I am greatly disturbed—in a quandary," confided a friend, "about this matter of forgiveness. Years ago, I suffered at the hands of a person whom I *thought* I had forgiven. As time goes on, however, the whole situation crosses my mind. It happens infrequently, but it *does* happen. If I have truly forgiven this person, what is wrong? Why do I have these thoughts? What can I do about them? God's Word tells me that I need to forgive others their trespasses as He forgives mine, so why should I remember the offense? Doesn't He forgive and forget our sins?"

Her predicament haunted me. I began to search the Scriptures for answers. Asaph, writer of Psalm 79, pleads with the Lord in Verse 8: "Oh, do not *remember* former iniquities against us! Let Your tender mercies come speedily to meet us, For we have been brought very low." This is the cry of every generation. In Hebrews 8:11-12, the Lord vows that He will make a new covenant with Israel and the house of Judah during which time "all shall know Me, from the least of them to the greatest of them. For I will be merciful to their unrighteousness, and their sins and their lawless deeds I will remember no more." He repeats in Hebrews 10:17, "Their sins and their lawless deeds will I remember no more." He *remembers* them no more. Therein lays the key.

Does God forget? No. He does something better. He simply *does not remember* our sins. *Elohim*, the God of creation, made us in His image. Scientists claim that our minds are like mini-computers; everything we ever saw or heard is registered somewhere in our craniums—our brain boxes. It may not appear that way as we scratch our heads trying to figure out where we dropped our shoes last night, or what we had for breakfast this morning, but that is merely because we cannot always bring to the forefront those things that are hidden in the recesses of our minds.

"I, even I, am He who blots out your transgressions for My own sake; And I will not remember your sins" (Isaiah 43:25). God's Word tells us that He forgives us for His sake as well as ours. What an incentive! We know that harboring resentment or bitterness provokes any number of ailments ranging from arthritis to colitis to mental illness. So it behooves us to forgive others, not only for Jesus' sake, but for our own well being. That person whom we have not forgiven actually has control of our lives. We have relinquished our peace of mind over to him/her. We actually become enslaved to the one whom we have not forgiven. We need to be aware that feelings and forgiveness have very little to do with one another. "Feelings come and feelings go and feelings are deceiving. My warrant is the Word of God; naught else is worth believing," said Martin Luther. Forgiveness is an act of the will. Once we have obeyed God, feelings usually "catch up." To forgive means to "send off or put away." Someone has given us a lovely portrayal of this: "Forgiveness is the Fragrance that the rose sends back to the heel that treads upon it."

June Hunt offered this formula for forgiveness on one of her radio broadcasts:

1. Confess the Hate. Be totally honest with yourself and God.
2. Confirm the Hurt. Don't camouflage it.
3. Choose to Heal. Decide to forgive.
4. Come to Harmony. You may never be able to reconcile with your offender, but you must come to harmony with your circumstances, those around you and God.

God has removed our sins from us "as far as the east is from the west" (see Psalm l03:l2). There is no boundary between east and west; it is limitless. So when memories of an old wound (once forgiven) "sting" your mind, don't fret. Just say: "Be gone! I've forgiven him/her." Then replace the thoughts with a Scripture verse or a praise song and *"remember them no more."* That's what God does.

Fruit That Remains

"I planted the seed, Apollos watered it, but God made it grow. So neither he who plants nor he who waters is anything, but only God, who makes things grow. The man who plants and the man who waters have one purpose, and each will be rewarded according to his own labor."

(1 Corinthians 3:6-8 NIV)

P robably the most exciting time in life is that moment when we are given the honor of leading a soul from spiritual blindness over the threshold into a personal relationship and a new life in Jesus Christ. There may have been others that diligently prayed for that person while someone else actually sowed the seed. Another then watered that seed before God chooses one of us to "reap a harvest where we have not sown." Such a privilege was that of Horace Snyder, former New Tribes missionary to Bolivia. He planted then his son took up the challenge and has ministered there for over forty years. He has eight other children who live to glorify God in various parts of the world. This particular account involves Mr. Snyder's son-in-law, Ed.

The story of Ed Jr.'s life was featured on the radio during the well known "Unshackled" program, stories from the Pacific Garden Mission, about men and women who were in bondage to sin and have found their way out. Ed's life as a youngster was miserable, although he was from an upper middle class Southern family. His father, a wicked promiscuous man, lived a double life, attending church on Sunday, but inflicting impossible demands on his family all week long. Ed became a handy prey for his dad's cruelty. One day he demanded that the boy be home from his sister's, a distance of two miles in ten minutes. "Or I'll beat the tar out of you, and don't you dare accept a ride," he bellowed over the phone. Admittedly, there were other factors involved in the boy's downfall, but parental abuse played a vital part in the road to ruin which Ed chose.

Marriage to his school sweetheart produced a daughter, but ended in divorce. After a hitch in the Vietnam War, he joined the Hari-Krishna sect, where he literally lost touch with reality. After several incarcerations in mental institutions and jails, he roamed aimlessly about the country like an animal for years. Disheveled, half-starved, not having had a personal conversation with any human being for seven years, he was befriended by a man who gave him lodging and urged him on the road to recovery. Ed, like King Nebuchadnezzar (Daniel 4:3l-34), experienced a metamorphosis. As he sought God, His animal heart was replaced with a Godly heart.

Years later, Ed has a positive relationship with his daughter, and now a lovely granddaughter. God has given him a Christian wife, Grace. Together, they live to further the Kingdom, handing out tracts, presenting Scripture on bill boards, and witnessing in many ways to those who might not otherwise learn of a salvation so rich and free.

"The Lord is …longsuffering toward us, not willing that any should perish, but that all should come to repentance."

(2 Peter 3:9)

Garden of Your Heart

"The Lord God planted a garden eastward in Eden, and there He put the man whom He had formed. And out of the ground the Lord God made every tree grow that is pleasant to the sight and good for food. The tree of life was also in the midst of the garden, and the tree of the knowledge of good and evil." (Genesis 2:8-9)

God planted the first garden, Eden (i.e. "delight" or "pleasantness") in the area of Babylon, a land we know as Iraq, for the benefit of mankind. Though tarnished by sin, it served as a model for generations to follow. A quiet spot, where one can find rest, solace and nourishment; the garden becomes a place of retreat for the soul.

Charles H. Spurgeon observed, "The heart of the believer is Christ's garden." It is ours to cultivate; to nourish characteristics that will please the Lord and bless others. In order for the fruit of the Spirit—love, joy, peace, patience, gentleness, goodness, faithfulness, and self-control to grow profusely, we must guard our heart's garden against the weeds of envy, selfishness, anger, bitterness, etc. Weeds are an unwanted commodity. Like poison ivy or poison oak that is obnoxious intruders in any garden, these unwelcome guests will ultimately take up residence in our hearts. Their function, once they are lodged there, is to contaminate healthy growth and destroy what the Holy Spirit desires to produce.

We are admonished to, "Put on the whole armor of God, that you may be able to stand against the 'wiles' of the devil" (Ephesians 6:11). The word "wiles" denotes a scheme; a specific method. The process is always the same. First, the destructive roots of envy and anger begin to crowd out the roots of love and peace that were planted by the Holy Spirit, using the devil's well-known "divide and conquer" strategy. Then a silent struggle ensues as those undesirable weeds begin to devour the soil's essential nutrients, causing healthy, sound plants to starve.

Finally, if left unchecked, weeds will grow tall enough to overshadow fruitful plants, and those which are deprived of the sun's (Son's) rays will wither and die. With the exception of a few shade plants, sunshine is essential to the growth and survival of a garden. A garden left unattended yields nothing but weeds. Let us guard our hearts so that none of those pesky weeds—envy, anger, bitterness, etc.—will take over.

We have a choice. We can *choose* to pluck out subversive roots *before* they become firmly entrenched. "Looking carefully lest anyone fall short of the grace of God; lest any root of bitterness springing up cause trouble, and by this many become defiled" (Hebrews 12:15). Not only we, but *others will* become defiled. Instead, since what we have is 'catching,' let's be contagious Christians. "If you extend your *soul* to the hungry and satisfy the afflicted soul, then...the Lord will guide you continually, and satisfy your *soul in* drought, and strengthen your bones; You shall be like a 'watered *garden,'* and *like* a spring of water, whose waters do not fail" (Isaiah 58:10-11).

Blessed Assurance! Our soul —heart—the seat of our emotions—will be "like a watered garden."

Rendezvous

My garden spoke to me today And breathed of things I scarce can say; Daffodils: Tender and sweet; yet gay and bold; You borrow from sunshine and give me pure gold.Red Poppy: You rakish one, wagging your head; Proclaiming: "Tis Springtime! Wake up! Winter's dead!" Pansy: Softer than velvet, you dear pansy face, With pensive, sweet smile, giving new shadows chase. Pink Rosebuds: Though fallen and crushed 'neath my feet,Send up fragrance of pardon; forgiveness is sweet. My garden is God's precious gift to me;

Grown to share - that all may see; 'Tis rather like a well loved book That warms the hearts of those who look. But the quiet peace that settles things, The deeper-than-the-petals things, O lovely tryst was made for three; My Garden – and My Lord – and me. "Their soul shall be as a watered garden; and they shall not sorrow any more at all."(Jeremiah 31:12b)

God of Comfort – God of Peace

❖

"Blessed be the God and Father of our Lord Jesus Christ, the Father of mercies and 'God of all comfort,' who comforts us in all our tribulation so that we will be able to comfort those who are in any trouble with the comfort with which we ourselves are comforted by God…" (2 Corinthians 1:3-4)

God of all Comfort: God is the *source* of all comfort. While it is true that a friend can offer us some degree of solace when we are hurting; cheer us up a bit when we are down; smooth our "ruffled feathers," God is the source of it all. If we are encouraged amidst our troubles and afflictions, we can be sure that later we will know how to console others who are suffering. We probably won't realize it while we are hurting because pain consumes all of our thinking, but once we begin to mend, God has a way of sending other wounded souls into our lives. It is not just for *our* good that God comforts us. Notice that the Apostle Paul says: "God…comforts us in all our affliction '*so that*' we will be able to comfort those..." A vital part of the equation is that when others are stressed, we will know – experientially – how to help them and how to console them in their hour of suffering.

Whatever the cause or our pain, if we are living to please God we will find real consolation in His Word and mercy from the "Father of Mercies" (2 Corinthians 1:3). It is our privilege and responsibility to encourage and help one another, applying Scriptures that relate to the wounded, and sharing the wisdom we have gained from them. To whom do we turn for Godly counsel and guidance? It is usually to someone who is familiar with the Word of God, especially one who has "been there," probably having dealt with a similar situation. A good student-learner of trial and testing becomes a good teacher of the same. A vital part of the purpose in our trial is that we may develop sound character and a deeper relationship with the God of all comfort so that we may be equipped to pass it on.

Hebrews 4:16 bids us "...come boldly unto the throne of grace, that we my obtain mercy, and find grace to help in time of need." We might translate loosely, "Go to the throne before the phone." Good idea. God's Word comes first and is the *source* of our consolation. "Whatever things were written before were written for our learning, that we through the patience and 'comfort of the Scriptures' might have hope" (Romans 15:4).

However, it is often a trusted friend/confidante who will point out Scriptures that have helped him/her in a time of testing, an hour of trial. And in sharing God's Word, the same comfort with which they were comforted, is "fleshed" out to the friend whose life may be in crisis, or who may just need a shoulder to lean upon. Sympathy is usually helpful, but we can offer *empathy* to another when we have experienced the same emotions through a similar trial of our own. God comforts us in all our affliction so we will be able to comfort those who are in any affliction with the comfort with which we ourselves are comforted by God.

God of Peace: Jesus said, "These things I have spoken to you, that in Me you may have *peace*. In the world you will have tribulation, but be of good cheer. I have overcome the world" (John 16:33). Previous to this time, Jesus had introduced the disciples to the Holy Spirit (Comforter, Advocate, Helper), promising them that He (the Spirit of Truth) would teach them all things and would be with them always (John 14:15-26). "Peace I leave with you, My peace I give to you; not as the world gives do I give to you. Let not your heart be troubled, neither let it be afraid" (John 14:27).

We were never promised a cessation of trouble in this world of turmoil and strife. But we do have the assurance that if and when we lose our sense of peace, we may turn to God and

He will fill us with all joy and peace as we trust Him, through the power of the Holy Ghost (paraphrase of Romans 15:13).

"And the 'God of peace' will crush Satan under your feet shortly" (Romans 16:20). That the God of *peace* would *crush* Satan under His feet would seem like a dichotomy except that in Genesis 3:15 this was the first prophecy that God made concerning Christ and His crucifixion. "And I will put enmity between you (Satan) and the woman, and between your seed and her Seed; He (Christ) shall bruise your head and you shall bruise His heel." This is the only historical reference to the woman's Seed.

The Apostle Paul exhorts us; "Finally, my brethren, whatever things are true, ...noble... just...pure...lovely... of good report, if there is any virtue and if there is anything praiseworthy—meditate on these things. The things which you learned and received and heard and saw in me, these do, and the 'God of peace' will be with you" (Philippians 4:8-9).

Then in Hebrews 13:20-21 it says, "Now the 'God of peace', who brought up our Lord Jesus from the dead, that great Shepherd of the sheep, through the blood of the everlasting covenant, make you complete in every good work to do His will."

The *first* thing that Jesus said to the disciples after He was resurrected was, "Peace be with you." After He had shown them His hands and sides, *again* He said, "Peace to you."

Eight days later, when He appeared to the disciples and Thomas behind locked doors, Jesus said for the third time, "Peace to you!" (John 20:19-26). Just as the 'God of peace' was involved in the resurrection of Jesus Christ, so will He be in ours.

If we submit to the 'God of peace,' He will make us holy so that our entire being—body, soul and spirit—may be presented faultless to Jesus when He comes. Our worries about being ready will be over.

"Now may the 'God of peace' Himself sanctify you completely; and may your whole spirit, soul and body be preserved blameless at the coming of our Lord Jesus Christ. He who calls you is faithful, who also will do it"

(1Thessalonians 5:23-24).

God of the Darkness

"But no one says, 'Where is God my Maker, who gives songs in the night?'" (Job 35:10)

Where is God when the lights go out? Job complained that men groan and their souls cry out against their oppressors, but to no avail. Have those ever been your sentiments? His friend, Elihu, reminds him that God is not at fault—that He is ready to comfort us when we weep and sometimes wail, if our hearts are penitent and laden with grace. His point is well taken. Even though some cry out in agony, God may not answer because of the pride and arrogance of evil and wicked men. (Job 35:9-13). Sometimes we lash out at God in anger because of a hardship, possibly a tragedy that we don't understand. That's what Job did. His friend accused him, and rightly so, of speaking "empty talk: words without knowledge."

Asaph, author of Psalm 73, also went through a time of despair when he did not understand why proud, wicked men were at ease and their riches increased while he, who had clean hands and a pure heart, was being chastened—until—"I went into the sanctuary of God; Then I understood their end" (vs. 17). His approach changed from horizontal to vertical; from man's *out-look to God's up-look. He* understood *that God would deal with the wicked in His time.* His hope was restored and he was renewed. That is what happens when we enter the "sanctuary of God." Our minds are cleansed and our hearts are lifted as we realize anew that God is in control. The darkness will be dispelled by the dawn. It has always been and will always be.

One unlikely source of encouragement can be found on an automobile license plate which reads: "GOD WORKS THE NIGHT SHIFT." At times we forget that. Many of the Psalms begin with despair only to end in victory when the focus turns from "self" to God. We find comfort in the Psalms because they point us from darkness to deliverance. "Why are you cast down, O my soul? And why are you disquieted within me? Hope in God, for I shall yet praise Him for the help of His countenance" (Psalm 42:5). Why worry when we can pray? When we praise God, we enter into His presence—into His sanctuary. It is impossible to worry and offer praise at the same time.

"But I will hope continually, and will praise You yet more and more." (Psalm 71:14)

God's Waiting Room

"I waited patiently for the Lord; And He inclined to me and heard my cry." (Psalm 40:1)

In all probability, the key words in Psalm 40:1 are "waited" and "patiently." They stem from the same Hebrew word "qavah," which means "to bind together-by twisting"—as though we might become a part of the woof and warp threaded through God's overall plan. Another part of the meaning is to "expect, to look for, to tarry, or wait upon." Waiting is not an easy assignment. The Holy Spirit gives us the call to serve but sometimes we are called upon to wait. Both are a vital part of the Lord's service. When we receive marching orders for a particular task, we are often given instructions as to where to go and what to do. But God's waiting room is more mysterious. We wonder: Why is this happening? How long will this take? What could it possibly be accomplishing for the Kingdom? Have I misread the map? It is difficult to persevere while we are in a "waiting mode," much less to do it "patiently." But God listens to our prayers. At times He "waits patiently" while we try to squirm our way out of a predicament. But when we are better able to *accept* our lot, He—in His time—relieves us.

Is there a doctor in the house? Most of us have spent time in the reception room of a doctor's office waiting for a diagnosis, hoping for the best. We fidget. With an eye on the clock, we thumb through the latest issue of "Time" or "Newsweek" in an effort to keep our minds occupied with something besides the reason we are there. We might whisper a prayer for mercy or peace but for the most part, the wait is not a pleasurable experience. The doctor is probably not intricately involved in our lives and furthermore, he probably does not even know we are there. We are just a name on a waiting list until the nurse calls for us to come into his office.

God, however, knows exactly where we are in His waiting room from the very beginning; and He has given us the "Bible" to read while we wait. Poet John Milton (1655) rightly observed: "They also serve who only stand and wait."

God's desire is to be involved with us; teaching us, comforting us, building character as our faith deepens. He is preparing us for healing or for a home in heaven, or both. It is this "binding together through twisting as with a rope" process that entwines our will with His will; that binds our individual spirit with the Holy Spirit. Such a cord is not easily broken.

Time spent in God's waiting room is usually according to God's plan, not our own. Think about it. Do you know anyone who is *not* waiting for an answer to prayer? Aren't you? We can follow our natural instinct to be anxious or we may place our trust in Him; the One who is in control and who has a plan for our lives. "For I know the thoughts that I think toward you, says the Lord, thoughts of peace and not of evil, to give you a future and a hope. Then you will call upon me and go and pray to Me, and I will listen to you. And you will seek Me and find Me, when you search for Me with all your heart" (Jeremiah 29:11-13).

Amy Carmichael, born in Ireland in 1867, later served in the dark land of India without a furlough for fifty-six years. She saved countless little boys and girls from temple prostitution, risking her life daily. Only God knows how many Indians were saved through her ministry. Falling into an unmarked pit left by construction workers, she was injured so severely that she became bedridden and never recovered from her plight. For the next thirty years, she was never without pain. Those who suffer through no fault of their own will identify with her honest appraisal of emotions that "flip-flop" but always end with an expectant hope. Is it any wonder that her writings—"Rose from Brier," "Though the Mountains Shake," "Candles in the Dark," or her winsome poem, "If"—all born of pain and suffering, have encouraged so many hurting souls? These gems that still bless people of all ages were birthed in *God's Waiting Room.*

You may not have heard of David Brainard. He was born in 1718 and orphaned at an early age. He contracted tuberculosis while a student at Yale. Extenuating circumstances kept him from becoming a pastor, his life's dream. He suffered with poor health along with what was then known as "melancholy." We call it depression. His zeal, however, was unparalleled and he became a missionary to Native Americans in New York State, Pennsylvania, and New Jersey. He led over one hundred Iroquois Indians of the Susquehanna Valley to the Lord over a two-year period and helped to start a school and a church. In 1747, at age twenty-nine, he died of tuberculosis even as his fiancée, Mary Edwards, (daughter of Jonathan Edwards of the Great Awakening) nursed him. His diary, "The Life of David Brainerd," is still in print, having helped shape the lives of John Wesley, Andrew Murray, William Carey, Jim Eliot and countless others. He lived in obscurity—in God's waiting room—all but two years of his life, but the seed that was sown has borne much fruit, the kind of fruit that remains (see John15:16).

"Trust in the Lord with all thine heart; and lean not unto thine own understanding. In all thy ways acknowledge Him and He shall direct thy paths" (Proverbs 3:5-6 KJV). There are times when we seem to be put on "hold." We feel as though we are in limbo. Actually, we are not. God is not on vacation. It may take months or even years of waiting in God's waiting room for God's decision. Meanwhile, we have a good book (the Bible) to meditate on while we wait. In our hustle and bustle existence, we want quick answers. But even when we do not get an immediate answer to prayer, we can rest assured that God is working something *in us* which He will later work out *through us.* God does not discipline out of a capricious mindset. The time is not wasted. He is God. He is love. He is good.

"The Lord will perfect that which concerns me. Your Mercy, O Lord, endures forever." (Psalm 138:8)

Grace – Sufficient, Abundant, Amazing

✤

"For by grace you have been saved through faith, and that not of yourselves, it is the gift of God, not of works lest any one should boast." (Ephesians 2:8-9)

It is by <u>grace</u> that we are saved—nothing else. Faith is an important part of our salvation, for it is "through" that faith which God bestows upon us that we first experience a taste of God's gift of grace. But in order to understand it, and make full use of it, we must gradually grow in it. "But grow in the grace and knowledge of our Lord and Savior, Jesus Christ" (2 Peter 3:18). Knowledge without grace can be risky. Knowledge "puffs up, but love edifies" (1 Corinthians 8:1b). Grace plus knowledge plus love equals a healthy balance.

Grace is the freely given, unmerited favor and love of God. It is derived from the Greek word "charis" meaning to bestow pleasure or delight. It is different from mercy. Mercy is God's divine favor and blessing bestowed on us when we definitely do _not_ deserve it. We do not deserve grace either. Grace is the freely given, unmerited favor and love of God. It has been said that anything this side of hell is pure grace.

We may know believers who live on the ragged edge, exercising an unbridled use of freedom now that they are secure in God's promise of eternal life. Perhaps we have behaved unseemly, knowing that what we were doing was not pleasing to God, thus deliberately taking advantage of our position in Christ. We might have assumed an attitude of indifference toward those in need, fudged on our income tax, or we may have committed blatant sin. Any time we deliberately take advantage of our salvation, using Jesus' death on the cross as merely an escape hatch and a fire-escape from hell, we are defying grace, whether we realize it or not. True, it is God's grace that forgives and keeps on forgiving. His supply is unlimited. But He did not save us by grace so that we could live in _dis_-grace. Charles Spurgeon said, "Grace is the mother and nurse of holiness; grace is _not_ an apologist of sin."

Most of us have witnessed the life of a friend or relative that has been shattered by sin and we shake our heads and say, "But by the *grace* of God, there go I." Do we realize what we are saying? Probably not. Most of us have no idea of the pitfalls we've narrowly missed, nor the self-imposed disaster that might have been our lot because we have taken for granted this gift. Grace is the gift that keeps on giving. It is limitless. It has no measure. It is sufficient.

The Apostle Paul pleaded with the Lord three times that his "thorn in the flesh" might depart from him. God's response: "And He said to me, My *grace* is sufficient for you; for My strength is made perfect in weakness" (2 Corinthians 12:9). What more could we ask? In our weakest moments God's strength is perfected (completed). Our infirmities, our handicaps are never wasted. His grace is sufficient.

The Apostle Paul begins almost every epistle with the salutation: "Grace and peace be unto you from God." We notice that grace proceeds peace and for a good reason. There is no measure of peace without grace; we can't have one without the other. Peter considered grace and peace of primary importance, too. He wrote in 1 Peter 1:2, "Grace to you and peace be 'multiplied.'" And in his second letter he adds, "Grace and peace be 'multiplied' to you in the knowledge of God" (2 Peter 1:2). The word 'multiplied' signifies a great abundance of both. James, the brother of Jesus, alludes to the grace of God in James Chapter 4, warning us to beware of covetousness and lust. He reminds us that to be a friend of the world is to be an enemy of God. But he encourages us saying, "God resists the proud, but gives grace to the humble" (James 4:6). We learn by experience that God gives in proportion to our need—not a stockpile for future use, but just enough for the moment.

"God has saved us and called us with a holy calling not according to our works, but according to His own purpose and 'grace' which was given to us in Christ Jesus 'before time began'…" (2 Timothy 1:9). We are saved by grace and grace will lead us Home.

God's Riches At Christ's Expense

Hedges – God's Boundaries

❖

"You have hedged me behind and before, and laid your hand upon me, such knowledge is too wonderful for me; it is high." (Psalm 139:5-6)

All of us are like sheep; we have gone astray (see Isaiah 53:6). There is none righteous; no, not one (see Romans 3:10). But GOD...who is rich in mercy and love toward us... comes to our rescue time and again by way of a *hedge*— either to hem us in, or to keep the world out, or both. However, it is always with the purpose of protecting us from the enemy. There are times when God stops us from taking action which would be harmful if carried out. His restraints are for our good but we don't always appreciate them.

For instance, God had protected Job who was considered "blameless and upright" before satan was given an opportunity to deal with him. Satan was familiar with *hedges*, asking God, "Have you not made a *hedge* around him (Job) and around his household and around all that he has on every side?" (Job 1:10). Whereupon God allowed satan temporary access to Job and his household; the rest is history. Although Job never really learned why God had tested him so severely, the result was that he grew stronger spiritually to a point where he could testify: "Though He slay me, yet will I trust in Him" (Job 13:15). "I have heard of you by the hearing of the ear; but now my eye sees You" (Job 42:5). God knew when to remove Job's hedge and when it was time to restore it. "And the Lord restored Job's loses when he prayed for his friends" (Job 42:10).

Boundaries: We all need boundaries – lines of demarcation. Recently, an experiment was performed on a group of small children who visited a large recreation park regularly. This park was surrounded by fencing on all sides. The children became so familiar with their appointed boundaries that when the fences were removed, not one of them strayed beyond the designated playground area which had kept them safe for months. Inadvertently, they had learned to respect their hedges, and were thereby kept from potential harm.

Our neighbor installed an electric fence around his property to keep his Black Lab dog from running away. You may have one of these fences in your yard. He allowed "Bo" to be "zapped" slightly just once. One day he disconnected the apparatus with the idea of testing the dog. When "Bo" approached the area where the fence had been electrified, he never ventured beyond a healthy distance from it. Mission accomplished – his yard became a safe haven. Even dogs have a healthy respect for boundaries. They live longer and better lives with restraints and so do we.

God's *hedges* of protection play a key role in Psalm 80. It is a prayer for revival following Israel's departure from the faith. It might well be a prayer for America in the 21st century. The Psalmist cries out, "Restore us, O God; Cause Your face to shine, and we shall be saved!" (Psalm 80:3, 7, 19). The Psalmist depicts Israel as a "vine out of Egypt" when she became a mighty, prosperous nation. Israel had obviously been "hedged in" and protected. "Why have You broken down her *hedges* so that all who pass by the way pluck her fruit?" cries the Psalmist (Psalm 80:12). When we no longer fear God, when we are not only in *the world but also* of *the world*, God may rightly remove our *hedge* of protection by way of disciplining us until our relationship with Him is restored.

God also reserves the right to build a *hedge* of thorns. When He dealt with Israel, (comparing her to the prophet Hosea's adulterous wife), He denounced her behavior and said: "Therefore, behold, I will hedge up your way with thorns and wall her in, so that she cannot find her paths" (Hosea 2:6). This "hedge of thorns" was for Israel's good. It prevented her from chasing after her lovers and straying outside healthy boundaries. As with Bo and his electric fence, the thorns kept Israel inside a safety zone, even though for her it was a painful experience. Can you think of a time when you desperately wanted a certain job you didn't get; wished to move elsewhere but couldn't; longed for a particular vacation but "circumstances" kept you from your desire? Apparently, God had other plans. We would probably be astounded if we realized the number of times that God has kept *us* from disaster by the invisible *hedges* He has placed around us.

"See, I have inscribed you on the palms of my hands; your walls are continually before me." (Isaiah 49:16)

He Knows

"And God said to him in a dream, 'Yes, I *know* that you did this in the integrity of your heart. For I also withheld you from sinning against me...'" (Genesis 20:6)

D oes it help to know that in the midst of toil and turmoil, God *knows* all about it? He *knows* about the terminal illness, the slander, the persecution for the cause of justice, that precious child who is "different," those panic attacks and the enemy's devious, diabolical schemes. He knows.

The Old Testament patriarch Abraham, who was to become the father of many nations, set out for a new land with his wife, Sarah. In those days it was not uncommon for a man to be killed; and his wife, if she was beautiful, stolen from him. In order to protect himself, he told King Abimelech a *little white lie.* "She is my sister." It was the second time he had used this little "trick" (see Genesis 12:10-20), thinking his life might be in danger.

How many of us learn the hard way? Abraham lied, (withheld some of the truth) and Sarah swore by it (see Genesis 20:5). Abimelech took her into his harem, but not into his bed. Then God came to the king in a dream and told him: "Indeed you are a dead man because of the woman whom you have taken, for she is a man's wife" (Genesis 20:3). Did you ever wonder where the expression originated, "If you do this or that," referring to some wrong doing, "you are dead"? It was here.

Now God was well aware of Abimelech's good intentions, so He protected him from a disastrous mistake. God came before the king in a dream and said: "Yes, I *know* that you did this in the integrity of your heart. For I also withheld you from sinning against me; therefore I did not let you touch her" (Genesis 20:6). God knew. There are several lessons contained within this scenario—a true story—but most remarkable is the fact that: "He *knows* our hearts." Shouldn't that encourage and console us?

Man's "bent" has always been to *know* more, beginning with the Tower of Babel when people decided, "come, let us build ourselves a city, and a tower whose top is in the heavens; let us make a name for ourselves lest we be scattered abroad over the face of the whole earth" (Genesis 11:4). God's Word tells us to gain as much knowledge as we like as long as it is used for good: "Wise people store up knowledge" (Proverbs

10:14). "The prudent are crowned with knowledge" (Proverbs 14:18).

A recent development, the result of man's ongoing quest "to *know,*" has resulted in a satellite system whereby the owner of an automobile can send an S.O.S. from any place to the dealership from whom he purchased his car. Then, using a pre-programmed code, the car is immediately located. Doors may be unlocked, lights turned on, and if more help is needed, it will be provided. The satellite knows where the vehicle is stationed at all times.

Yet man's technology is child's play compared to God's knowledge. God is *omniscient*—"omni" meaning "all" and "scient" from which we get our words "knowing" and "science." Scientists generally agree that everything is governed by time, force, action, space and matter. Genesis 1:1 tells us: "In the beginning"—time; "God"—force; "created"—action; "the heavens"—space; "and the earth"—matter. God is omniscient.

God is also omnipotent; all powerful, almighty; Master over land and sea. Romans 1:20 speaks of "His eternal power and Godhead." God is omnipresent which simply means that He is present everywhere. He told Joshua: "Be strong and of good courage; do not be afraid, nor be dismayed, for the Lord your God is with you *wherever* you go" (Joshua 1:9). The Psalmist asks a rhetorical question: "Where can I flee from Your presence?" (see Psalm 139:1-7). Implied answer: "Nowhere."

Unlike those satellite systems that are being perfected, our Lord has not only complete awareness but an *understanding* of our whereabouts. "For we have not an high priest which cannot be touched with the feeling of our infirmities (weaknesses); but was in all points tempted like as we are, yet without sin" (Hebrews 4:15 KJV). He *knows* our feelings. He *knows* His sheep (John 10:14, 27, 28), and promises them eternal life. He *knows* those who are His (2 Timothy 2:19). When God *knows*, He also *understands* completely, based on a personal relationship with us. He *knows our* needs even before we ask and teaches us to pray for them (Matthew 6:8-13). He *knows* our hearts. He *knows and cares.*

"But He *knows* the way that I take; when He has tested me, I shall come forth as gold." (Job 23:10)

Hope

"Looking for the blessed *hope* and glorious appearing of our great God and Savior Jesus Christ." (Titus 2:13)

It was a custom in years past, for a young man who was engaged to gift his fiancée with a large cedar-lined box called a "hope chest." Eventually, it would be filled with many beautiful hand-crafted items for use when the bride and groom established a home. Some were gifts, some family heirlooms, some fragile and others durable, but each one was a treasure. The hope chest, of course, was a token based on the "hope" that the couple would live happily ever after. Now we identify the word "hope" with a rather uncertain outcome. We use it when actually there is very little *of* it. The farmer pines: "I *hope* it doesn't rain until after the harvest." A mother, clutching her little boy's hand, cautions: "That dog looks ferocious; I hope he doesn't bite." It's a mediocre hope at best. But when hope is used in the Scriptures, it almost always stems from words meaning "an expected end" or "a sure thing."

For example, Psalms 42:5, 11 and Psalm 43:5 we read: "*Hope* in God" from a root word in Hebrew meaning "to wait with hope" on Him who never fails. These verses are based on the assurance of God's help in the face of discouragement or sorrow or pain. "Hope in God for I shall yet praise Him for the help of his countenance" (Psalm 42:5; 42:11). We are urged to place our "hope in God" three consecutive times in these two Psalms, which would indicate that it is worth our special attention. The idea of "hope" here refers to "a favorable and confident expectation," something on which we can hang our faith. Regardless of our circumstances, He *will* help us and we shall yet praise Him.

Faith that will triumph in times of trouble is ours for the taking by virtue of the *hope* that God has given us. We are called to "rejoice in *hope* of the glory of God. And not only that, but we glory in tribulations, knowing that tribulation produces perseverance (patience) and perseverance, character, and character, *hope*" (Romans 5:1-5). Each trial is like a tunnel that we go through and come out on the other end. We are told that trouble "produces" something. It tests our patience, which builds our character, and we can *hope* again because we have seen how God brought us through the trial—our tunnel.

The Apostle Paul, in Romans 8:23 24, refers to believers who are waiting for the redemption of their bodies. "For we were saved in this *hope* but *hope* that is seen is not *hope;* for why does one still *hope* for what he sees? But if we *hope* for that which we do not see, we eagerly wait for it with perseverance." Here, the original Greek word used is "elpis," which means to "anticipate with pleasure, with expectation, and with confidence." In other words, a sure thing. When we actually experience the redemption of our bodies; we will *be* in Heaven with Jesus. The *hope* that we have now will be realized. There will be no more need for it. As the Apostle Paul says, "Why does one still *hope* for what he sees?" If we could see our future, there would be no need for *hope.* "Beloved, now we are children of God; and it has not yet been revealed what we shall be, but we know that when He is revealed, we shall be like Him, for we shall see Him as He is. And everyone who has this *hope* in him purifies himself; just as He is pure" (1 John 3:1-3). We shall be like Him. Amazing! We become more like Him, becoming pure by just clinging to this *hope*—by mere association. "In *hope* of eternal life which God, who cannot lie, promised before time began" (Titus 1:2).

Hope is a lot like salvation. It is really a gift from God. There is nothing we can do to acquire it, except believe God. We can't work to make it happen. But if we continually *believe* that God will do what He says He will do, hope will become a part of us. It is our choice. We merely need to believe His Word and stake our claim on the *hope* that He has offered.

Dr. Roger Hinrichs, Professor of Nuclear Physics, said: "God's love is not always found in our circumstances, but His 'hope' is always there."

Man can live thirty days without food and three days without water, but he cannot really *live* one day without hope.

"May the God of *hope* fill you with joy and peace, in believing, that you may abound in *hope* through the power of the Holy Spirit." (Romans 15:13)

Instruments of God

"Praise the Lord with the harp; Make melody to Him with an instrument of ten strings." (Psalm 33:2)

Something to ponder: The ten-stringed harp, dedicated to the Lord, made sweet music. Each of us has been blessed with ten fingers and ten toes–barring an accident or some irregularity. Our hands represent our work and we have ten fingers with which to pursue it. "And let the beauty and delightfulness and favor of the Lord our God be upon us: confirm and establish the work of our hands—yes, the work of our hands, confirm and establish it" (Psalm 90:17 AMP). Each finger has fourteen finger bones, assorted tendons, and twenty-five thousand nerve endings per square centimeter. The potential for creating with these digits is mind boggling. We may use our hands (with ten fingers) to produce many beautiful and delightful works on behalf of our Lord God.

Our feet have ten toes and they take us where we are going. They determine our walk. It may be on the path that God has chosen for us (the road less traveled) or *our* way, the highway. "Enter by the narrow gate; for wide is the gate and broad is the way that leads to destruction, and there are many who go in by it. Because narrow is the gate and difficult is the way which leads to life, and there are few who find it" (Matthew 7:13-14). Jesus also said, "I am the light of the world. He who follows Me shall *not* walk in darkness, but have the light of life" (John 8:12). The choice is ours. David, in the midst of hopelessness and depression prayed, "Cause me to hear Your loving-kindness in the morning, for in You do I trust; Cause me to know the way in which I should walk; for I lift up my soul to You" (Psalm 143:8). God's answer to that prayer is bound to point us in the right direction.

Alvin Vandergriend, in his book "Love to Pray," notes that when we *pray* we are "instruments of God." Of course, our hearts must be "in tune" with His in order for Him to use us. As instruments, we point out specific needs (God already knows what they are) whereupon He focuses on those needs and answers our prayers according to His will. The Apostle Paul was very specific as he admonished us, "Do not present your members as *instruments* of unrighteousness to sin, but present yourselves to God as being alive from the dead, and your members as *instruments* of righteousness to God" (Romans

6:13 emphasis added). Paul practiced what he preached. As an instrument of righteousness, God "used" him mightily. He yielded his members to God and became the instrument that the Holy Spirit used to write the epistles: Galatians, Ephesians, Philippians, and Colossians. He also became the first missionary—heralding the Good News (the Gospel) as he planted churches in most of the civilized world.

One gentleman, a retired technology teacher who owns a four-hundred-acre tree farm, uses the scraps of his red cedars when they are felled in a way that the Lord can't help but be pleased with. He creates wooden fish enhanced by a cross in the middle, making a lovely gift that includes a salvation tract in a small folder for others to hand out to the unsaved. Over five thousand of these little cedar fish and tracts have been distributed and only God knows how many souls have been saved as a result. Both the hands which make these treasures and the feet of those who carry them are God's "instruments."

So let us offer our members to become instruments of righteousness unto God. Once we have yielded, it is reassuring to realize that whatever we do, whether it be mundane or magnificent, God will use it for His glory to further the Kingdom. We will bring harmony with our "ten stringed instruments" to a discordant world.

"For we are His workmanship, created in Christ Jesus for good works, which God prepared beforehand that we should walk in them." (Ephesians 2:10)

I Will

"Forgetting those things which are behind, and reaching forward to those things which are ahead, I press toward the goal for the prize of the upward call of God in Christ Jesus." (Philippians 3:13-14)

It's that time again! Thousands of people will gather and sing "Auld Lang Syne," as the big ball at New York City's Times Square is lowered on the stroke of midnight, signaling the end of the old and ushering in the New Year. We may regret, even resent the swiftness of time passing, but there is an aura of magic about hanging up a brand new calendar; watching the Rose Bowl Parade and the Super Bowl game; and of course, making those New Year's Resolutions. They are the most magical of all, often disappearing with a flick of the wrist. We make and break them with amazing dexterity.

W. Glyn Evans, in his "Daily With the King," states that we make decisions based either on the seat of our emotions or the heart of our will. We choose. He writes: "Our emotions are as dessert to the spirit within us, tasty but not substantive, whereas the will is the 'steak and potatoes' of the Christian life."

Long ago, Lucifer became a fallen angel, the result of a misdirected will. According to Isaiah 14:13-14, he said in his heart,

1. I will ascend into heaven.
2. I will exalt my throne above the stars of God.
3. I will sit also upon the mount of the congregation on the farthest sides of the north.
4. I will ascend above the heights of the clouds.
5. I will be like the most High.

Does all this sound like New Age? It's really old age. Obviously, these are not goals that we would strive for. Yet there is a higher road than "resolutions" open to us. We may align the "heart of our will" with that of the Psalmist as in Psalm ll6:l-l7 and be guaranteed a closer walk with God this coming year.

1. I will call upon Him as long as I live (see verse 2).
2. I will walk before the Lord (see verse 9).
3. I will take the cup of salvation (see verse 13).
4. I will pay my vows to the Lord (see verse 18).
5. I will offer to You the sacrifice of thanksgiving (see verse 17).

Let's hide these concepts in our hearts, and ask the Holy Spirit to bring them to mind daily. When we do, God will be glorified and we can look forward to an extraordinary, blessed New Year.

"Beloved, I pray that you may prosper in all things and be in health, just as your soul prospers." (3 John 2)

Joy

❖

"Now may the God of hope fill you with all **joy** and peace in believing, that you may abound in hope by the power of the Holy Spirit." (Romans 15:13)

"Create in me a clean heart, O God, and renew a steadfast spirit within me. Do not cast me away from Your presence, and do not take your Holy Spirit from me. Restore to me the **joy** of Your salvation, and uphold me by Your generous Spirit" (Psalm 51:10-12). This was the cry of King David's heart after his sin—that of committing adultery with Bathsheba—had found him out.

Have you ever temporarily lost the joy of your salvation? If you have, do you know the reason why? Perhaps it seems like ages since you have experienced genuine joy. We do not expect to be bubbly and deliriously happy all the time. But when that deep-down, underneath-the-surface feeling of "dis-ease" engulfs us and we know we are in trouble, we don't need to remain there. God never planned it that way. There is a balm in Gilead. The pain may be real, but the misery is optional.

We may not have indulged in any gross sin. Perhaps we have kept short, honest accounts with God and our slate is—for all intents and purposes—fairly clean. Yet, some element is missing. There are times when we can't put a finger on the cause of our discontent. Our walk and our talk are not really synchronized as they once were. We seem to be "out of synch." A friend calls it "dissonance"—a lack of harmony or a discordant note in the "symphony" of life. Do we realize that joy is ours for the taking? It is. God's Word says so. "Now may the God of hope fill you with all **joy** and peace in believing, that you may abound in hope by the power of the Holy Spirit" (Romans 15:13).

Many references to the "joy" that is at our disposal in the Word of God are just bursting with the promise to replace our veil of gloom with a covering of cheer. During Jesus' discourse on the vine and the branches in the 15th Chapter of John, He taught His disciples that if they would abide (dwell) in Him, and His words abide in them, they would bear much fruit, glorify the Father, and they would receive answers to their prayers (see John 15:5-8). He urged them to abide in His love, adding, "These things I have spoken to you, so that My **joy** may remain in you, and that your **joy** may be full" (John

15:11). God assures us that knowing what He has spoken and acting upon it to the best of our ability—abiding in the vine—is a warranty for fullness of "joy."

So what has happened? What if we have delved into God's Word regularly attempting to apply it to our lives, and we are still void of the joy that we seek? "The fruit of the spirit is love, joy, peace..." (Galatians 5:22). What happened? What are we missing? A small "catch-phrase" (no irreverence intended) in Romans 15:13 holds the key. The God of hope will fill us with joy and peace "in believing" or as the NIV renders it, "as you trust Him." It is as simple as that. It was unbelief or lack of trust that kept God's people, the Israelites, from entering the Promised Land thousands of years ago.

The Lord had led them out of Egypt and through the Red Sea; then He directed them to capture that "land of milk and honey," the Promised Land (Exodus 3:8). Moses scolded them, "Yet in spite of this word you did not believe (trust, rely on, and remain steadfast to) the Lord your God" (Deuteronomy 1:32 AMP). Dr. Adrian Rogers said: "It took one day to get Israel out of Egypt; but it took forty years to get Egypt out of Israel."

We have reacted to God's Word in the same way that the Israelites did. It is really that we have not believed nor trusted Him that our joy is "short-circuited." Either we trust God and believe His Word—or not. Nehemiah 8:10 tells us, "The **joy** of the Lord is your strength." It is not a warm, fuzzy feeling. The word "strength" here indicates a "fortified place or defense." We rarely attribute to "joy" the stronghold that it is. It is difficult for the enemy—that old serpent—to gain entry when joy is our fortress. Joy is not found in the absence of trouble, but in the presence of God. Mark Twain said, "Grief can take care of itself, but to get the full value of a joy you must have somebody to divide it with."[1] So share your **joy**!

"And you became followers of us and of the Lord, having received the word in much affliction, with **joy** of the Holy Spirit, so that you became examples to all in Macedonia and Achaia who believe." (1 Thessalonians 1:6-7)

[1] Famousquotes.com/Mark Twain/joyone space

Joy Follows Obedience

"Though He were a Son, yet He learned obedience by the things which He suffered." (Hebrews 5:8)

"Looking unto Jesus, the author and finisher of our faith; who for the **joy** that was set before Him endured the cross, despising the shame, and has sat down at the right hand of the throne of God." (Hebrews 12:2)

The day was half over. I had flitted from chore to chore without accomplishing anything. My mind and spirit were ill at ease. Where was the joy that Jesus spoke of in John? "If you keep My commandments, you shall abide in My love...These things I have spoken to you, that My joy might remain in you, and that your joy may be full" (John 15:10-11). Depression was settling in. I cried out to God and then I called my prayer partner who agreed to intercede on my behalf. Several hours later a problem I had "stuffed" surfaced.

I had felt the sting of betrayal some time ago and the wound was still "smarting." Instead of forgiving and trusting God for the outcome, I had been spinning a web of fear and anxiety. The door of my mind had been left open to the enemy allowing him to rob me of my joy.

Here was the key. The answer was obvious—not easy, but obvious. "For if you forgive men their trespasses, your heavenly Father will also forgive you" (Matthew 6:14).I knew from past experience how it worked. If I forgive the "offender" by word of mouth—an act of the will, eventually my heart and emotions would catch up. By that one act of obedience, I could expect, like King David of old, a renewed spirit and the restoration of the joy of my salvation (see Psalm 51:10-12). I surrendered. By evening, I was sensing the victory that was already mine. "But thanks be to God, who gives us the victory through our Lord Jesus Christ" (1 Corinthian 15:57).

Of course, forgiveness does not always come that quickly, but once a decision is made, the healing begins. Two days later as I encountered that individual, I was pleasantly aware of a new freedom in our friendship. We exchanged warm smiles and hugs; our friendship would continue at a deeper level. God had answered my prayer. I had come full circle; from withholding forgiveness—to obedience—to a heart full of joy. As always, Jesus led the way.

"Who for the joy that was set before Him endured the cross, despising the shame, and has sat down at the right hand of the throne of God" (Hebrews 12:2). For the believer, joy follows obedience as surely as night follows day.

Just the Right Size

❖

"Jesus said …Most assuredly, I say to you, I am the door of the sheep. All who ever came before Me are thieves and robbers…I am the door. If anyone enters by Me, he will be saved." (John 10:9)

"You don't understand!" protested the young man, "I've done such terrible things in the past! God could not possibly forgive them all. It's too late for me to be saved." He sincerely believed that his sins were so great—his problems so big—that God's grace was not sufficient to cover them.

This, in direct contrast to the elderly couple who have regularly attended church for years. Their neighbors admire them for their kindness. They have operated a successful business and raised a lovely family. They are *good* people who say, "Our God is a God of love. He would never allow anyone to go to hell (if there were one)." "We have sinned," they admit, "but we have not done anything so wicked as to condemn us to hell. We will meet in Heaven no doubt." They believe that their sins are so small and insignificant that God would not refuse them entrance into Heaven. They cannot fathom that, "There is none righteous, no not one" (Romans 3:10). "Whoever shall keep the whole law and yet stumble in one point, he is guilty of all" (James 2:10).

Long, long ago when the world was spiritually much as it is today—very corrupt—God instructed Noah to build an ark for the salvation of Noah and his family. The Ark was large enough to accommodate every kind of animal, by twos and sevens, to come aboard. We find in Chapter six of Genesis, explicit measurements for the ark: length, width, breadth, height, even for the windows.

In verses fourteen to sixteen, Noah was told to build it four hundred-fifty feet long, seventy-five feet wide and forty-five feet high. The roof was to be finished to within eighteen inches of the top, with a door in the side and to make lower, middle and upper decks. A reliable source states that it was equivalent to more than five hundred standard American railroad stock cars, probably five hundred-seventy modern railroad cattle cars. Most experts agree that the Ark had approximately one million five hundred thousand cubic feet of space. That would have supported forty thousand animals, which would have required less than thirty percent of the Ark's space. That would have left seventy percent of the Ark's space free for animal supplies, Noah's family, food and personal belongings. These figures can be found in "Popular Issues – Learn more about the size of Noah's Ark."

But no amount of searching reveals a specified size for the door. "…you shall set the door of the ark in its side" (Genesis 6:16). We do not know its size, but we do know that it accommodated animals of every species, both large and small. It was just the "right" size. …" And the Lord shut him in and closed (the door) round about him" (Genesis 7:16 Amp).

Jesus said, "I am the door; if anyone enters in by Me, he will be saved and will go in and out and find pasture" (John 10:9). Anyone…no matter the size of his/her sin…Jesus is our "door." He is our entrance into Heaven, the perfect dimension for your sins and mine; just the right size. God provided an ark for Noah's temporal salvation. He gave us His only begotten Son for our eternal salvation.

We raise our voices to Annie Johnson Flint's, "His love has no limit; His grace has no measure; His power has no boundary known unto men." Our children sing lustily, "One Door, and only one, and yet its sides are two; I'm on the inside; on which side are you?" Beloved, let us make sure we are on the "right" side of the Door that measures just the "right" size for you and me.

Jesus said: "I am the Door. If anyone enters by Me, he will be saved…" (John 10:9).

Lean Into the Rock

"And all drank the same spiritual drink. For they drank of
that spiritual Rock that followed them; and that Rock was
Christ." (1 Corinthians 10:4)

This portion of Corinthians refers to the Israelites during
their Exodus from Egypt. "Their drink was a stream
fetched from a Rock which followed them in all their journey-
ing in the wilderness; and this Rock was Christ, that is, in type
and figure" (Matthew Henry). Throughout Scripture, both in
the Old and New Testaments, we find "rock" used metaphor-
ically in describing our relationship to God and vice versa.
"The LORD is my rock, and my fortress and my deliverer; the
God of my strength, in whom I will trust..." (2 Samuel 22:2-3
and Psalm 18:2). The Bible is ripe with references such as
these, which give us the quiet, calm assurance that comes
with knowing Jesus as our Rock.

White water rafting is becoming an increasingly popular form of recreation for Americans. Almost every state in the U.S. now advertises vacation spots where people can enjoy this water sport. The Salmon and Snake Rivers in Idaho are among the favorite vacation spots for those hardy souls who seek to combine excitement with relaxation in their leisure hours. Rafting satisfies the need for developing mental and physical acumen, while it offers thrills and surprises peculiar to white water. There is one motto—slogan—password among rafters. When they encounter turbulent waters and find themselves being twisted and tossed out of control, they must always "lean into" the wave, or "lean toward" the rock, to avoid disaster. "Lean into the rock!" is the common cry.

A rock in the path of water rushing down stream diverts the water around it, causing the water to build up higher along the rocks' surface, picking up speed because of the increased volume flowing around the rock. This extra speed, along with the greater volume and height of the water, forces the raft away from the rock. Consequently, rocks are often "people friendly" to rafters. By leaning into the rocks instead of frantically trying to paddle away from them, the guiding current can swiftly and efficiently navigate the raft safely past the threats and fears. In the volume of life, that obstacle which appears to be threatening and dangerous may actually provide the necessary force to move us safely along the path.

Many Old Testament Scriptures encourage us to "trust" in the Lord. Some of them mean to put confidence in; to wait; be patient; to hope; to take refuge. However, there is the recurring theme of one particular word which is translated "trust." The Hebrew word "batach" means to literally flee for refuge, to be bold, even careless, but confident and secure; to lean on; to trust. The Lord comforted Zion, reminding His people: "My righteousness is near, My salvation has gone forth, and My arms shall judge the peoples; the coastlands will wait upon Me, and on My arm they will trust" (Isaiah 51:5).

We are instructed in Proverbs 3:5 to, "Trust in the Lord with all your heart; and lean not on your own understanding." We are to lean toward—lean into our Rock. And that Rock is Christ.

Legacy of a Friend

❖

"Ointment and perfume rejoice the heart: so doth the sweetness of a man's friend by hearty counsel."

(Proverbs 27:9 KJV)

Her name was Mary Agnes Wagner. Born in 1907, saved at age 4, she gave her first testimony before a gathering at a Mission House and several men were saved. Newspaper headlines, some of them three inches high, in the states of Massachusetts, Connecticut, New Hampshire, Rhode Island, New York as well as much of the northwest, bore witness to the fact that this young girl was set apart for service to the King. At nine years of age, she testified of Jesus Christ and His power to save at a prison. Hard-hearted men were so broken in spirit, that they nearly fell over one another in approaching the altar, crying out to be led to a saving knowledge of the Lord.

Her messages crossed denominational lines. When she was twelve years old, A. B. Simpson, Founder of the Christian and Missionary Alliance Church, assured that she possessed a singular anointing, dedicated Mary Agnes to the Lord's service in Old Orchard Park, Maine. God's plan was unfolding, a life designed to be unequivocally yielded to Him until the time of her Home-going at the age of ninety-three.

Her husband, Paul, was the highly respected principal of a large high school and in her words, "Priest in our home," though she may have been more versed in the Bible than he. Her Sunday School classes often numbered well over 200 men and women who longed to know God better. She mentored and discipled countless women, teaching and admonishing them to reverence God and love their families; to be submissive wives and chaste keepers of their homes (according to Titus 2:3-5), that the Word of God might not be dishonored. She was a unique embodiment of the Proverbs 31 lady.

She usually prayed the Scriptures. One of her ten grandchildren recalled how she had consistently prayed Colossians 1:9-14 over her family asking, "that you may be filled with the knowledge of His will in all wisdom and spiritual understanding; that you may walk worthy of the Lord, fully pleasing Him, being fruitful in every good work and increasing in the knowledge of God, strengthened with all might, according to His glorious power, for all patience and longsuffering with joy;

giving thanks to the Father who has qualified us to be partakers of the inheritance of the saints in the light. He has delivered us from the power of darkness and conveyed us into the kingdom of the Son of His love, in whom we have redemption through His blood, the forgiveness of sins."

What do you suppose would happen if we prayed this Scripture, or Ephesians 1:15-21, or perhaps Ephesians 3:14-20, or Philippians 1:3-6 on a regular basis on behalf of our children and theirs? Can you think of a finer legacy? Her entire family bears witness to God's faithfulness to hear and answer such entreaty. Mary Agnes had three children: Margie Van Antwerp, Ginny Obergfell and Paul Wagner, who founded New Covenant Church of Oswego, New York and Believers' Chapel in Syracuse. As Dr. Charles Stanley expresses it, "These prayers are in accordance with God's will; He can't *help* but answer them."

"Charm is deceitful and beauty is passing, but a woman who fears the Lord, she shall be praised. Give her of the fruit of her hands, and let her own works praise her in the gates." (Proverbs 31:30-31)

Lessons from the Red Bird

✤

"Look at the birds of the air, for they neither sow nor reap nor gather into barns; yet your heavenly Father feeds them. Are you not of more value than they?" (Matthew 6:26)

Our Heavenly Father does care for our fine feathered friends. Then, there are those inquisitive souls who feed them year in and year out for the sheer pleasure of becoming familiar with various birds, and their "family" traditions. They are called "birders." It shouldn't surprise us to find that God endowed each species with its own coterie—a kind of clique—with specific rules and regulations, much like that of other creatures, including humans.

For instance, those tiny black and white Chickadees will eagerly wait for one another at a feeder, honoring their militaristic pecking system. Although these little creatures are extremely friendly, the "General" usually feeds while the

"Colonel" and the "Sergeant" dutifully await their turn, according to rank and file.

Goldfinches, those gaily decorated yellow songbirds with black and white wing stripes, are voracious eaters and very aggressively drive other small birds away. Each species has its peculiar traits but the beautiful crested red cardinal demonstrates some of the most unique behavioral patterns of all.

For several winter/summer cycles, we were captivated by a one-legged cardinal and his mate. This gorgeous red bird whom we called, "Hop-a-long," and his equally lovely (if a bit subdued) mate, "Mrs. C," beguiled us with their intriguing approach to life and each other. First of all, they are of the families that mate for life. Divorce rate = 0%. Invariably, the female is encouraged to feed first, while the male keeps vigil on a nearby branch or spot on the ground. Because of her muted coloring, the female is less likely to be spotted by a marauding predator. When one of the pair is feeding, we can assume that the other is diligently watching close by. The pair often passes sunflower seeds to one another, beak to beak, sharing their bounty and submitting to one another. Perhaps because they are the most timid of all, they will be the first ones to come to a feeder at dawn and the last to feed at night.

Philippians 2:4 tells us, "Let each of you look out not only for his own interests, but also for the interests of others." Are we mortals not advised to submit to one another "in the fear of God" (see Ephesians 5:2I)? A display of pathos captured our attention one winter, when Mrs. C. flew into our neighbor's bay window and broke her neck. Hop-a-long mourned her death the entire season. He refused food for days at a time, and would sit dejectedly at our feeder for hours. His heart was obviously broken. It was pitiful. We thought he was about to die, until one fine day in spring he appeared bringing with him a sleek, younger model. (Isn't that just like a man?) He had acquired a new warble, a new mate, a new beginning. God gave man dominion over the birds of the air though they were created first (see Genesis 1:21-22, 28 2:19-20).

Isn't it conceivable that we might consider the cardinal an object lesson to remind us that God desires that we cherish and care for one another in a lifetime commitment?

"Even the sparrow has found a home, and the swallow a nest for herself" (Psalm 84:3). Therefore, each of us who are "bound in the bundle of life" with God as our refuge (see I Samuel 25:29), esteem highly our earthly nest and those within, praising and thanking God for the privilege of loving one another.

Life - (A Series of Parentheses)

> "To everything there is a season…A time to weep, And a time to laugh; A time to gain, And a time to lose; A time to keep, And a time to throw away; A time to keep silence, And a time to speak"... (Ecclesiastes 3:1-7)

Seasons; periods; phases; *parentheses.* "It's just a *phase*" has been the time-worn *excuse* for every *inexcusable* behavior from pulling Patty's pigtails when you were seven, to offensive personal hygiene ("I just *had* a bath on Saturday") at thirteen. Mothers use the, "Oh, it's just a phase" phrase to maintain their sanity while the kids are growing up. No matter what life holds for mom—she may be a wife, career woman, and/or an "executive household manager"—most of her attention is diverted toward her children while she is raising them. Bearing and rearing them constitutes a *parenthesis* in her life. Ironically, by the time she has earned an honorary degree in the science of behavioral modification, they have all grown up and left home. Ask any mother, however, and she will affirm this as a very special, meaningful part of her life.

One such landmark stands out in my mind during the B.C. (before Christ)period of my life when I took time out from a frenzied pace to "entertain" a nervous breakdown. Neither tears nor cajoling had changed the will of the only God I knew—the God who did things *my* way—and I was disillusioned. Life was not what I expected; this wasn't "happily ever after." Then my best friend—my Dad—died, and for three years I nourished a spirit of bitterness, which culminated in clinical depression. That was a low point. This three year *parenthesis* ended with good news as this was God's way of drawing me to Himself.

"Then you will call upon Me and go and pray to Me, and I will listen to you. And you will seek Me and find Me, when you search for Me with all your heart" (Jeremiah 29:12, 13). Finding God the Father, through Jesus Christ, will forever stand out as the high point in my life.

Your "phases" may revolve around a childhood happening; college years; when you learned ceramics; oil painting; karate; the year you built your dream house or completed the marathon. Then there are those events over which we have no control—loss of a spouse, a child; a job; empty nest syndrome; a broken relationship. Times of sickness and sadness bring to mind the old saying, "Life gets tedious, doesn't it?" But it is really just another opportunity to trust God. A friend who had just begun college learned that her mother was suffering from cancer and was terminally ill. She immediately left school and went home to care for her beloved Mom. Upon returning to complete her studies, she reflected that this had been a sad but gratifying experience, a *parenthesis*, within her college years. Is your heart heavy today? God knew it would be. Trust Him.

Remember, this will pass. One phase moves out as another phase moves in. Some bring joy and others bring sorrow. Every end is a new beginning. This may seem to be redundant, but it is not. There are many "new" beginnings in a life time.

Abraham Lincoln was a man whose life was stalked by discouragement. He had experienced failure in business, politics, and romance. He was forced to declare bankruptcy; suffered defeat in the political arena; and mourned the death of his young fiancée a short time before their appointed wedding date. Yet, in later years, he reflected that, "a man is just about as happy as he makes up his mind to be."

Life is a series of adjustments, a revolving door of experiences, and each one with potential for enriching our lives. It is more exciting when we take note of the beautiful flowers along the path and listen for the sound of the birds. Live well; love much; laugh often. Practice "koinonia" (fellowship), whenever possible. Whatever a day or a year brings forth, there is yet another *parenthesis* just around the corner. Life is a journey not a destination.

"This is the day that the Lord has made; we will rejoice and be glad in it." (Psalm 118:24)

Love One Another

"But earnestly desire the greater gifts. And I show you a still more excellent way." (Corinthians 12:31 NAS)

Among a small group of people, our hostess asked: "If you could name the two most important things about your walk with God, what would they be?" Within a few seconds I heard myself say, "love" and "hope," in that order. What would your answer be? Peace, Comfort, Love, Joy? What makes your world go 'round?The Apostle Paul teaches us about spiritual gifts in 1 Corinthians 12—gifts of service, wisdom, faith, healing, etc., all given by the Holy Spirit. In verse 31 he says, "And I show you a still more excellent way" (NAS). The word "way" means a route, a road, a journey. People will say, "It's easy for some people to love others—I just don't have that gift." But love is not a gift. It is a higher "way" for our sojourn. Have you ever noticed the number of times God tells us to "love one another" in His Word? "One loving heart sets another on fire," according to St. Augustine.

Love is a fruit of the Spirit according to Galatians 5:22. It is listed as the "first" fruit. "How can I love everybody?" asked a friend, "It just isn't working for me." Although there are no pat answers, it is possible. God spells it out for us in His Word. Jesus said, "Truly, truly, I say to you, unless a grain of wheat falls into the earth and dies, it remains alone; but if it dies, it bears much fruit" (John 12:24 NAS). So we see that whatever fruit we bear must come from dying to self—not by doing. It is only then that the fruit of the Spirit takes root, sprouts and produces: love, joy, peace, patience, kindness, goodness and faithfulness (see Galatians 5:22). God's love is borne of dying, not doing. We cannot produce love by our will.

True love, "agape," is a decision. It is a choice. It does not rise and fall with the tide, or depend on a warm, fuzzy feeling. It may *involve* our emotions but it does not *depend* upon them. Martin Luther has said: "Feelings come and feelings go; and feelings are deceiving. My warrant is the Word of God; naught else is worth believing." We may not "feel" like loving that "irregular person" right now but there is hope. Have you ever prayed, "God, love him/her *through me*?"

Try it. Let go and let God do it. In Matthew 5:43-44 Jesus said, "You have heard it said, 'You shall love your neighbor and hate your enemy.' But I say to you, love your enemies, bless those who curse you. Do good to those who hate you, and pray for those who spitefully use you and persecute you..." How can we possibly <u>love</u> someone we don't even <u>like</u>? We can because Jesus gives us the formula in Matthew 5:44.

1. "Bless" that person. Say something kind to or about him/her.

2. "Do something good." Love is a verb which means it requires action. If your specialty is baking, make a pie to share with him/her. If not baking, then find another way to bless them like offer to baby sit or send a little encouraging note. Allow your creativity to be your guide. Scientists claim that when we do something "good" and are involved in a "giving behavior," certain chemicals are produced in our bodies that result in greater tranquility, joy and trust—even a diminishing of chronic aches and pains. Doing good also helps us sleep better at night.

3. "Pray" for those who spitefully use you. Do you bring someone whom you are not particularly fond of before the Lord in sincere prayer? It is virtually impossible to intercede consistently for another without   eventually forming an emotional attachment. The hardness in our hearts will begin to soften.

Once we have determined to be obedient to God's Word, our emotions usually "catch up." We may love the "irregular" person whom God has placed in our lives, in spite of ourselves. The best way to destroy our enemies is to make them our friends.

"You also, as living stones, are being built up a spiritual house, a holy priesthood...acceptable to God through Jesus Christ" (1 Peter 2:5). And *love* is the grout that holds us together.

"By this shall all men will know that you are My disciples, if you have love for one another." (John 13:35)

Measure of Love

"For God so loved the world that He *gave*...His only begotten Son..." (John 3:16)

"**I**n the spring a young man's fancy lightly turns to thoughts of love," wrote the English poet, Alfred Lord Tennyson. The publisher of Tennyson's poems was said to have ordered an extra supply of the letters "l", "o", "v", and "e" whenever they printed Tennyson's poems because he used the word "love" so frequently. For centuries poets have heralded springtime as the season when, "a young man's fancy lightly turns to thoughts of love." Unfortunately, the love referred to here is more accurately described as romance; that "floating on a fluffy cloud" intangible feeling that is often mistaken for love, but may not be akin to it at all. While secular love is often sublime, it is usually temporary and not worthy to be compared to agape love which is God's love.

Not since the beginning of time, has there been a love like God's love. God is love (1 John 4:8). God the Father loved us enough that He gave His only begotten Son for us. Jesus loved us so much He willingly gave Himself—His all as a substitute for your sins and mine, to demonstrate—prove His love for us (Romans 5:8). God's agape love is measured by how much it has given.

The Apostle Paul calls into action each member of the Godhead in his prayer that we, the family of God, will understand and experience the love of God (Ephesians 3:13-21). He explains that his suffering was part of God's plan. He kneels before the Father of our Lord Jesus Christ, from whom we derive our name (family of God). He prays, "That we may be strengthened with might through the Holy Spirit in the inner man; and that Christ may dwell in our hearts through faith."

All this leads us to the focal point of our own walk of love. Paul prayed that we would all be, "rooted and established in love, may have power, together with all the saints, to grasp how 'wide' and 'long' and 'high' and 'deep' is the love of Christ, and to know this love which surpasses knowledge, that you may be filled to the measure of all the fullness of God" (Ephesians 3:17-19 NIV).

Once Christ lives in our hearts, we need to ponder the 'width' and 'length' - horizontal dimension; and the 'depth and 'height' - vertical dimension (although it is unfathomable);

before we can begin "to 'know experientially' the love of Christ which passes knowledge" (Ephesians 3:18-19).

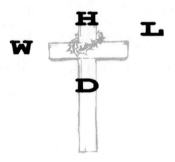

Our fine feathered friends serve as role models of sacrificial love. A mother eagle builds an eight foot by ten foot monstrous nest, which has been said to look like a bonfire waiting to happen. Upon its completion, according to radio speaker Mary Whelchel, the mother eagle will soften the nest by plucking "down" from her chest, which she arranges like fluffy accent pillows in a living room, providing her eaglet a comfy, cozy nest. She gives an offering from her own body; an offering of love to her eaglets. Even more remarkable is the dedication of the mother hornbill, named for her enormous megaphone-shaped beak. She lives deep in the rain forests of Africa. After she and her mate build a nest in the hollow of a tree, and cover the entrance with mud and dung, she turns her treacherous beak on her own body, plucking not just "down," but primary feathers, which render her unable to fly leaving her totally helpless. Why? She does this so that her hatchling will not be injured by the sharp shafts of these powerful feathers. How does one measure such love?

"Mercy and truth have met together; Righteousness and peace have kissed" (Psalm 85:10). The psalmist foretold of the love that would be displayed at the Cross. We could never presume to love as Christ loved. He loved so much that He gave His all. It was not the nails, but love that held our Savior to the tree. It is commonplace for people to give without loving, but it is utterly, totally incomprehensible to love without giving. A bell is not a bell until it is rung; a song is not a song until it is sung; love is not love until it is given away. And we can never out give God.

"...Jesus knowing that His hour had come...having loved His own who were in the world, He loved them to the end."

(John 13:1 NAS)

Miracles

"For they had not understood about the loaves; for their heart was hardened." (Mark 6:52)

What is *a miracle?* Do you believe in them? Did they really happen? Do they still happen? Are they real? What difference does it make? How might they affect our lives? There are myriads of questions surrounding the mystery of *miracles.*

Jesus sent the twelve apostles forth, two by two, specifically to work "power over unclean spirits…And they cast out many demons, and anointed with oil many who were sick, and healed them" (Mark 6:7 &13). These men were commissioned to "work miracles," which they did. Soon thereafter Jesus fed five thousand people with two loaves of bread and five fish which a lad offered to share with the crowd that had assembled (see Mark 6:30-52). Without fanfare, Jesus blessed the loaves and the fish and divided them among the crowd. They all ate and were filled and there were twelve baskets left over! Five thousand men had eaten and who knows how many women and children! Talk about miracles!

But the effect on the disciples was short lived. Immediately after this miracle, Jesus "sent" these same disciples out into the sea where they encountered a storm at night. When Jesus came to them "walking on water," they panicked thinking it was a ghost. They had no recognition of Jesus at all! What difference had the miracle of the loaves made? Apparently, it was not enough. Mark 6:52 tells us that "they had not understood about the loaves, because their hearts were hardened."

What about you and me? Are our hearts so hard that we can't trust God to perform a miracle? Would we recognize one if we saw it? Have we been privy to a few of them without knowing it? The Apostle John lists several other miracles for us to ponder as well.

Jesus changed water into wine at Cana; healed countless people and made the blind to see. He healed a man who had suffered from an infirmity for thirty-eight years instructing the man to, "Rise, take up your bed and walk." Immediately, the man was made well. He came with his back on a bed and left with a bed on his back (see John 5:1-15). These are but a few of the recorded miracles of Jesus. The question we must answer now is do they still happen today?

Edith, a woman driving toward a dangerous turn called the "can of worms" in Upstate New York, was suddenly face to face with a six-wheeler bearing down on her, head on. She sent up an "arrow prayer" and does not remember a thing until seconds later when she found herself "deposited" on the road across the median, her car facing the opposite direction and out of harm's way. She says that she "blacked out" and wondered it if was an angel who took the wheel. We may never know, but Edith thanks God for the miracle that saved her life.

A little girl receives a missionary barrel containing a doll exactly like the one she had prayed for, from someone she will never know. Isn't that a miracle? Anita, a recently widowed lady, desperately needed her septic system repaired. Her basement was flooded but she had no money at all. The "Roto-rooter" people quoted her a price of $287.25. They agreed to come on Saturday. She prayed for help but none came until she went to her mailbox Saturday morning, where she found a check for exactly $287.25. It seems some people in a nearby church (not hers) heard of the widow's plight and had prayed for her during the previous Wednesday night prayer meeting. Someone there had just had carpet installed in a new home and the amount left over from the estimated price was $287.25. They felt led to bless this fellow believer, a total stranger, with the money. Wasn't that a miracle?

Tim and Shari had adopted Jelena, a teenage orphan from Latvia, after overcoming all the grueling legalities. Flying from Europe, they had a stopover in Atlanta, Georgia. They had dinner and freshened up. Jelena spoke no English so she would point out her needs. Since she was not familiar with western plumbing, her adoptive mother was obliged to help her in the restroom, and in so doing, left her purse hanging on a hook there. When they arrived home in New York, the purse was missing. They called explaining exactly where the purse could be found, but there was no record of it. The family searched their laundry. They searched high and low but to no avail. Shari was hysterical because of the legal documents she had lost. Finally, it was as though she heard a voice telling her, "Your job is to care for the orphans. Go to bed and rest." When she awoke the next morning, her purse was found in the same spot on a shelf where it had always been kept, just outside her bedroom door. No one knows how it got there. Wasn't that a miracle?

A young couple with two small children came to know the Lord while the husband was in graduate school. Their finances were very tight and they allotted only so much each week for groceries. The wife dreaded the time when her detergent would run out as that always meant a big chunk of her grocery money would have to go to replace it. As they were praying, trying to trust God for their finances, she noticed that the box of detergent never seemed to get to the end. Having read about the widow of Zarapheth in 1 Kings 17:7-16, this couple believed that God had done a similar miracle for them. As they used the detergent, God filled it back up to help meet their needs. Wasn't that a miracle?

Bob had been a Science Biology teacher for twenty-five years when he was suddenly stricken with multiple strokes. He suffered the complete loss of the use of one side, total loss of speech and memory. He could not even remember his son's name. After many weeks in a hospital, he was shifted to a rehabilitation unit where his family was told that, at the very best, he might eventually be able to "make his needs known." Doctors had done all they could. This teacher became a student again having to relearn his ABC's, read and write, walk, etc. God restored him and now, twenty years later, he is "Mr. Fix-it" at home and at his church, where he is also an elder. He and his wife, Nancy, are involved with missions. He is a devoted family man who serves the Lord with a heart of gratitude. One would never guess that he was incapacitated. Bob is a walking miracle.

David and Michelle, a young missionary couple with six children, serve with New Tribes in Papua, New Guinea. Their desire is to make the Word of God known to unreached people groups. When their last furlough was due, they were $7,000 short of the funds they would need to bring them back home.

Although they had never petitioned anyone for funds before, they finally wrote to their "sending church" requesting help. Before they posted the request, a letter came in the mail from an elderly member of that church who had known Michelle from the time she was a small child. He had just sold some land in Pennsylvania and felt led to send the proceeds to her family in New Guinea. The amount of the check was exactly $7,000. David never sent the letter. Another miracle?

The term "God hunt" was coined several years ago by Dr. David Mains, of Chapel of the Air. He challenged us to keep a daily record of the "little things" that we take for granted, as well as the big things. Recently, a 100 foot tree toppled by the wind, missed our house by a very narrow margin. Who but God? Practice hunting for Him daily, you may find His fingerprints in some very unexpected places.

"You will seek Me and find Me, when you search for Me with all your heart." (Jeremiah 29:13)

No Language Barrier

❖

"But the Lord came down to see the city and the tower which the sons of men had built. And the Lord said, 'Indeed the people are one and they all have one language.'"

(Genesis 11:5-6)

Our chairs formed a large circle in the lobby of the Salisbury Bible Institute in Pune (pronounced Poona), near Bombay in the state of Maharashtra, India. It was an uncomfortably hot summer afternoon in the plains. My friend, the hostess, had been called away so I was a minority of <u>one</u> seated amidst a sea of unfamiliar faces and tongues. Added to my discomfort (I was the only light skinned person there) was the fact that these people from halfway around the world were multi-lingual or at least bi-lingual. I was not. Feeling very much alone in the crowd, I focused my attention on my saree (gown) and the wrist bangles I was wearing, twisting and turning them in an effort to hide my embarrassment. My heart was thumping so loud that I was sure everyone could hear it.

When I finally dared raise my eyes, they fell on a dark skinned man sitting directly across the room, who wore a gleaming white "dohti," the typical two-piece village man's attire. He was smiling at me, the most dazzling smile I had ever seen. It was God's answer to my fears. My heart melted. Without a word, God's love had been translated from Telagu to English, and I had found a friend.

Though many years have passed since that time, a man from a remote village in India has inquired as to my well-being, and prayed for me and I for him. My friends from India have since emigrated to Canada and Virginia where they are an extension of God's love. We have become "family." "Blest be the tie that binds." There is no language barrier in a smile.

Have you ever tried smiling at those who glance your way as you walk in the mall? Responses will vary from an icy stare, to a perplexed "are you out of your mind?" expression, to an uneasy double-take, to a warm smile. Try it. I understand that while it takes seventy-two muscles to frown, it only takes fourteen muscles to smile. There is no language barrier in a smile. It is the same in any language. I used to smile in English, but now it's universal. How about you?

"Rejoice with those who rejoice and weep with those who weep" (Romans 12:15). There is no language barrier in grief but people approach it differently according to the culture in which they live. Years ago, while I was in the city of Bangalore, India, staying with Brother John Gollapalli, (of Far East Broadcasting) I received a puzzling message from a woman whom I had met at a prayer meeting a few days earlier. Her twenty-seven-year-old son, James, the apple of her eye, had died very suddenly and mysteriously. She asked if I would come to sit with her at the "viewing." My hosts informed me that this was the custom and an honor reserved for only a few. They strongly advised me to go. Despite a qualm or two, I took my place alongside this dear grief-stricken woman, not quite knowing what to expect.

Friends streamed in literally by the hundreds. Personnel from Youth for Christ and Far East Broadcasting Association ministered to the family. The atmosphere was charged with a spirit of victory and resurrection power. My new friend spoke almost no English and I knew very little Tamil. But she had reckoned with a truth that I had overlooked. A mother's heart is a mother's heart. We were part of an ancient custom and there would be no language barrier between us that evening. Grief is the same in any language. Thomas Aquinas said it best: "Witness at all times; if necessary, use words."

His dark eyes never left my face. He listened with rapt attention as I crooned Braham's Lullaby to the little four month old bundle of life that I carried in my arms. We strolled along the wrought-iron enclosed balcony adjoining a certain stucco house in Bangalore, India. Asheel, a baby boy, responded with a series of "coos" and "gurgles"—inflections in all the right places. It was a familiar syndrome. After all, I had heard the same sounds from my own children in America, years before. There is no language barrier in "baby talk." It is the same in any language.

I was reminded of that time in history before the Tower of Babel, when earth's entire population spoke one language. "Now the whole earth had one language and one speech" (Genesis 11:1). God, in His infinite wisdom, gave to babies a universal language—one that we can all understand.

One Day at a Time

❖

"Therefore do not worry about tomorrow, for tomorrow will worry about its own things. Sufficient for the day is its own trouble." (Matthew 6:34)

'Twas the week before Christmas and all through the house were strewn parts of paper angels, my favorite gift project of the season. I was doing exactly what I wanted to do, when I wanted to do it. Yet, my mind raced ahead, spinning ideas for any number of future activities. Presently, I realized how little enjoyment I was getting from this "fun thing" because I was concentrating so heavily on what was next on the agenda. It occurred to me that I had spent much of my life eagerly, if not anxiously awaiting what comes next.

When I was a little girl, dressing in "grown-up" clothes was my favorite "pretend" game. When someone asked how old I was, I remember saying, "I am four going on five." I could hardly wait for school days and was constantly struggling with: "What shall I be when I grow up?" Sound familiar? We look forward to the end of school and entering the work force. We equate age sixteen with obtaining a driver's license; then we accelerate toward twenty-one, which spells liberation from curfews. Some of us begin to dream of marriage, followed by children and grandchildren. Planning for the future is healthy, but living in the future can be debilitating.

I recalled a painting of lovely flowers bordering a path which I had seen recently at a friend's home. The caption read: "Happiness is found along the way, not at the end of the road." As that simple truth dawned on me, I began to pray, asking the Lord to help me savor each moment. As we simmer down and begin to take joy in doing simple things—even mundane things—life takes on a new dimension. Routine chores lose their drudgery, colors seem brighter, and "fun things" become fun.

It's been observed that experience is what we get while we are looking for something else. So, in order to reap the most joy from our sojourn here on earth, let's be content to live one day at a time. Whether holidays or ordinary days, each one becomes a special day, as we are mindful to thank God for the flowers along the path.

"This is the day the Lord has made; we will rejoice and be glad in it." (Psalm ll8:24)

On the Way

"Then the man bowed down his head and worshiped the Lord. And he said, 'Blessed be the Lord God of my master Abraham…As for me, being *on the way*, the Lord *led* me to the house of my master's brethren.' " (Genesis 24:26-27)

Eliezer, oldest servant of the patriarch Abraham, found himself in the right place, at the right time, doing the right thing as we delve into the story of his quest for a suitable wife for Abraham's son, Isaac. Wouldn't you like to know you are in the place where God can best use you, His servant, to help round out His kingdom during the coming years? Let's examine some of the ways that God has used to bring this about in the lives of others.

First, Eliezer was presented with an assignment to find a wife for Isaac (who is approximately 40 years old at this time) from among his own people, rather than the corrupt, idolatrous Canaanite women. Abraham assured his faithful servant that if the lady of his choice refused to join him, he would not be held responsible. It would be a long journey but God promised to send an angel before Eliezer. After careful consideration, he agreed to the search. He devised a plan, and the Bible tells us that while he was asking God for confirmation—"it happened, before he had finished speaking, Rebekah...came out with a pitcher on her shoulder" (Genesis 24:15). Nothing just "happens" in God's economy. Eliezer promptly thanked and praised God saying, "As for me, *being on the way,* the Lord *led* me to the house of my master's brethren" (Genesis 24:27). Rebekah would indeed become Isaac's wife.

At the time of the flood the Lord "was sorry that He had made man on the earth and He was grieved in His heart" (Genesis 6:6) because of man's violence and wickedness. He chose righteous Noah for a project that would take 120 years to complete. As he constructed the ark, Noah became a laughingstock but this was the vehicle God would use to preserve His people and civilization itself. His genealogy records that "Noah walked with God" (Genesis 6:9), bearing witness that He was also "*on the way.*"

The Old Testament Book of Ruth exemplifies selflessness and a relationship to God seldom equaled, while presenting one of the most beautiful love stories of the ages. Husbands of both Ruth and her mother-in-law, Naomi, had died in the pagan country of Moab, where they had lived for many years.

Leaving relatives and friends, Naomi chose to return to the land of Judah and to God's people, from whence she had come. She urged her daughters-in-law to remain amidst the security of their people and their gods, but Ruth elected to join Naomi, for better or worse. She would worship the God of Israel. They arrived at Bethlehem during the springtime of barley harvest, where Ruth volunteered to glean grain in the fields for their sustenance.

"She happened to come to the part of the field belonging to Boaz" (Ruth 2:3), a relative of her father-in-law. We smile at another "happenstance" but the fact remains, Ruth was "*on the way.*" Boaz treated her with utmost respect, later becoming her "kinsman redeemer." Widows were usually either ignored or mistreated in that culture. However, Ruth was destined, through their marriage, to become King David's great-grand-mother, figuring into the prophetic lineage of Jesus Christ.

The Apostle John received the vision that would become the Book of Revelation while he was "in the Spirit on the Lord's Day" (Revelation 1:10). Surely his exile to the Isle of Patmos was part of God's plan.

There is no coincidence in the life of a follower of Christ. Those "happenings" which we have noted were divine appointments. We may concede then, that if we walk faithfully in the place where God has placed us with no selfish hidden agenda, there is every reason to believe that one day, like

Eliezer, we will look back and muse: "I was 'on the way' and the Lord led me."

"The steps of a good man are ordered by the Lord."

(Psalm 37:23)

Palm Tree Christians

❖

"The righteous shall flourish like a palm tree, he will grow like a cedar in Lebanon. Those who are planted in the house of the LORD, shall flourish in the courts of our God. They shall still bear fruit in old age; they shall be fresh and flourishing…" (Psalm 92:12-14)

"Blessed is the man who trusts in the LORD, and whose hope is the Lord. For he shall be like a tree planted by the waters, which spreads out its roots by the river, and will not fear when heat comes; its leaf will be green: and will not be anxious in the year of drought, nor will cease from yielding fruit." (Jeremiah 17:7-8)

Psalm 92:12 refers to the date palm (Hebrew-"tamar"). It has to be planted and carefully tended when it is young; it never grows wild. It is different from other trees in that it grows from within. Its growing, living tissue is in a column in the center of the trunk. The bark can be removed, it can be scarred and cut, but still the palm grows up and up towards the sky. For the bark is only the support and protection of the inner life of the palm. The quality and quantity of its fruit are determined by the success of the growth of its inner life.

Do you see the comparison to the righteous? Those who trust in God? Our success in our Christian life is determined by our growth within. Our "outer man" is like the bark of the palm—we can be mistreated, marred and scarred by various circumstances, but if our inner self is healthy, nothing can retard our spiritual growth. Isn't that enough to make you shout? The Bible tells us: "And we know that God causes all things to work together for good to those who love God, to those who are called according to His purpose" (Romans 8:28). "Even though our outer man is perishing, yet the inward man is being renewed day by day" (2 Corinthians 4:16).

Then we learn that the palm has 360 uses, one for nearly every day in the year: food, timber, rope, cloth, baskets, mats, couches, brushes, brooms, shades and windbreakers. Its foliage is always green, for its roots extend far and deep into the earth taking advantage of hidden moisture. It thrives even in dry and sandy soil. What about us?

We, who call ourselves children of the King of kings and Lord of lords, should also be willing to be used in many different ways. Have you heard remarks like these? "If I can't teach that class, I don't want to teach at all!" or "If I can't be on the board or on the council I'll just sit back." They should add: "And pout." But not so with the *date palm* tree which is used both for food and as the lowly door mat. It does not wilt when water is withheld for a season, for its roots go deep.

How often do we Christians leave a revival full of vim and vigor, but after a few weeks have passed find we have become listless and dull. That's when we need to drive our roots down deep into the source of living water, God's Word Jesus Christ (John 4:14).

This next bit of information may be a glad surprise—the date palm bears its best fruit in old age! Its fruit is the sweetest and best when the palm is <u>eighty</u> years old! How about that? When an apple or an oak tree gets old, the apples and acorns get smaller and smaller and eventually they are worthless. By a nearby river stands a majestic old oak, probably one hundred years old. But its acorns are so tiny that even the squirrels reject them. Not so with the date palm; the older the tree, the better the fruit. Can you see why God likens us to this palm? The farther along we get in our Christian life, the sweeter we should become. How can we attain and maintain inner strength, and bear rich fruit as we grow older? Become a Palm Tree Christian!

"The righteous shall flourish like a palm tree."

(Psalm 92:12)

Planted—Not Hodge-Podge Growth

❖

"Blessed is the man who trusts in the LORD, and whose hope is the LORD. For he shall be like a tree *planted* by the waters, which spreads out its roots by the river, and will not fear when heat comes." (Jeremiah 17:7-8)

There it was, bursting exuberantly through its buds, its little old-fashioned daffodil blossoms swaying merrily back and forth in the April breeze, introducing us to spring. This was not part of a well-designed garden. Almost hidden beside tall grasses at the bottom of a small footbridge, this dwarfish plant had sprung up without a keeper's tender touch. A yellow harbinger of springtime, it warmed our hearts, but its obscure location posed a question. Who else would see it? Was its beauty being wasted? Have you ever thought that you might be *planted* in an unlikely spot or worse yet—you might just be a victim of *hodge-podge growth* as in —"What am I doing here"?

"Give ear and hear my voice..." God instructs the farmer (and us) with wisdom and discretion, teaching planting skills necessary for producing a bountiful harvest. Following the principle "precept upon precept, line upon line, here a little, there a little," we learn some essentials of agriculture and how to apply them to life (Isaiah 28). The questions: "Does the plowman keep plowing all day to sow? Does he keep turning his soil and breaking the clods?" (Isaiah 28:24). These questions are posed to make us think and there is only one answer, "No."

Obviously, not until after the soil is harrowed, cultivated and leveled off is it ready to be *planted* with seed. So it is with us. Only after some of the "clods" in our lives—hatred, contentions, jealousies, outbursts of wrath, adultery, idolatry are broken up, and we are leveled off, can the seed of God's Word be entrusted to us. Then we are fit to be *planted.* The farmer sows dill (fennel) and scatters cumin, (which has been superseded in modern times by caraway seeds). He then plants the wheat in neat rows because it produces the most yield that way. Barley is sown in its "appointed place." Barley and wheat are sown in October and November after the early rains, at an "appointed time." Finally, spelt (because it is a border plant) is *planted* where it can get the most sun. "For He instructs and teaches him in right judgment" (Isaiah 28:26).

Consider. Unless we have blatantly defied the Lord to arrive at our location, situation, etc. (present state of affairs), we may safely assume that He has *planted* us here, whether the harvest we yearn for be evidenced or not. Before we move on to the next assignment "the Lord of hosts, who is wonderful in counsel and excellent in guidance" (Isaiah 28:29), must complete the next phase in the growth process. The dill plant is not threshed with a sledge, (it is not necessary) nor is the cumin (caraway) run over by a cartwheel. This cartwheel consisted of a vehicle with sharp metal spikes on its wheels, which was used for separating *stubborn* grains from their hulls. It was called a "tribulum" from which we get our word "tribulation."

Have you undergone tribulation? God, in His wisdom and love for us, allows it sometimes to divest us of useless chaff. Dill was merely beaten with a staff or stick, and the cumin with a slightly more forceful tool, the rod. Bread flour must be ground (bruised), but not crushed, by either the cartwheel or its horsemen (Isaiah 28:27-29), because crushed it would have no value as food for souls. God knows precisely the measure of sunshine and rain each of His children needs for bearing fruit. Remember, He *planted* the first garden eastward of Eden.

For a time I pondered whether those lovely daffodils were the result of *hodge-podge* growth or a *planting* of the Lord. I am not sure. But one thing is certain. They were blooming as though they were *planted* and our hearts were blessed. We don't have to worry about *hodge-podge* growth. The Husbandman plants, prunes and harvests His own wisely. Dr. Adrian Rogers said: "It takes forty *days* to grow a squash; forty *years* to grow an oak." It usually takes forty years for the oak to produce an acorn.

"He desires that we may be called trees (oaks) of righteousness, the *planting* of the Lord, that He may be glorified." (Isaiah 61:3b)

Prescription for Eternal Youth

❖

"He gives power to the weak, And to those who have no might He increases strength. Even the youths shall faint and be weary, And the young men shall utterly fall, But those who wait on the Lord shall renew their strength; They shall mount up with wings like eagles, They shall run and not be weary, They shall walk and not faint." (Isaiah 40:31)

The word "wait" used here is from a Hebrew word meaning to bind together by twisting. It indicates that as our lives become intertwined with the Lord, our strength (or power, force) will continually be renewed—changed—as time goes on. Our *inward* man will be rejuvenated and our strength renewed as the occasion demands. We all have access to this unique spiritual journey. It can be ours.

People have always been on a quest for living long, happy lives. During early Biblical times, it is obvious that people lived longer, healthier lives than at any subsequent time period.

Methuselah, son of Enoch, lived 969 years; Noah, who built the ark, 950 years. Scientists theorize that previous to the Great Flood, earth's ozone layer was thicker and purer than at any time since, because there had been no rain from on high. Dew from the ground provided the necessary water. Water content in the atmosphere decreased drastically after the flood, with its forty days and forty nights of rain. The environment was much kinder, conducive to longer life spans than it is today. It is likely that atmospheric conditions will continue to deteriorate in the future on earth as we know it. Small wonder that people scoffed at Noah's 120 year effort in building the ark. First of all, he lived between the Tigris and Euphrates rivers on dry land and secondly, rain had never been a factor in their lives; it was unheard of.

Ponce de Leon, a Spanish explorer, born approximately 1460 (date uncertain), after sailing with Columbus on his second voyage to the Americas in 1493, began a search for the legendary Fountain of Youth some twenty years later. On behalf of King Ferdinand II of Spain, he landed on the east coast of Florida where he founded St. Augustine, North America's oldest city. There he found a prehistoric Indian Spring that he thought was an answer to the mystery of longevity. It was not. You may have visited the Fountain of Youth Archaeological Park there, and tasted water from that very Indian Spring. Did your health improve? No, the fabled Spring has *not* solved the problems encountered with aging. Ponce de Leon and his men treated American Indians with extreme brutality; raping and pillaging; sometimes wiping out entire villages. He reaped what he had sown when in the year 1521 he died of an arrow wound inflicted by a Native American; his hopes dashed, his life's dream unrealized.

Five centuries after his death, scientists are still doing research, hoping to unveil new secrets of longevity. Yet there *is* a prescription for eternal youth to the soul who *waits* on the Lord for strength. "Therefore we do not lose heart. Even though our *outward* man is perishing, yet the *inward* man is being renewed day by day" (2 Corinthians 4:16). This may or may not add years to your life, but it is guaranteed to add life to your years.

Prisoner of Hope

"Return to the stronghold, you prisoners of hope. Even today I declare that I will restore double to you."

(Zechariah 9:12)

Betty Mitchell and her husband Archie were Christian Missionary Alliance (CMA) missionaries to Vietnam that were taken captive during the Vietnam War. As they were being forced from the CMA headquarters by the Viet Cong, Betty's eyes fell on their open Bible to Zechariah 9:12. After the war she testified that she immediately tucked that message from God away in her heart, knowing that it was His way of preparing her for the uncertainty and the challenges of her future. Prisoners of war are forcibly subject to hostile treatment. Betty had no choice about that; yet she could and did choose to turn to her stronghold (Christ) as a place of refuge. That decision would set the tone not only for the period of her captivity, but for the rest of her life. She literally became a *"prisoner of hope."*

It seems incredible that any of us in our right minds would deliberately commit ourselves to any form of bondage. Still, any time we hang on to prejudice or entertain bitterness because we have been offended or cast a jaundiced eye of envy, we begin to build a barricade around our hearts. We figure that these boundaries will protect us from further hurt and pain. Instead they become impregnable walls of steel that bind unhealthy emotions within while restricting the Holy Spirit from teaching us to hope and trust in God. In order to partake of God's grace and look for deliverance from our self-inflicted prison of despair, we need to rid our minds of spiritual garbage, "...laying aside all malice, deceit, hypocrisy, envy and evil speaking..." (1 Peter 2:1). When we are caught in the web of discouragement, we can become *prisoners of hope* when we choose to turn to Christ as our stronghold.

In his very last letter to Timothy the Apostle Paul wrote, "Therefore do not be ashamed of the testimony of our Lord, nor of me His *prisoner*, but share with me in the sufferings for the gospel according to the power of God" (2 Timothy 1:8 emphasis added). Although Paul was facing imminent death, his famous last words show us he had that sure thing, that "hope" in the power and the glory of God. This hope did not disappoint him or make him ashamed to be called a prisoner of the Lord (see Romans 5:3-5). To be a prisoner of the Lord is to be a prisoner of hope. From a prison in Rome, Paul wrote: "I, therefore, the prisoner of the Lord, beseech you to walk worthy of the calling with which you were called" (Ephesians 4:1). All Christians are 'called' to that same hope – the hope of eternal life.

Betty Mitchell has lived a life worthy of her calling. Although she was released from the Vietnamese prison, her husband was not. He was never heard from again, still listed as a missing person. She has continued to serve the Lord throughout her life, a vessel unto honor. She has spoken to thousands of women who have been encouraged and blessed by her account of the faithfulness of the Lord, especially during those dreadful months following Archie's capture. She has become a role model for many suffering women. God kept the promise Betty read from Him in Zechariah 9:12, "I declare that I will restore double to you." Betty's daughter, Becki, a nurse, married Dr. David Thompson, a surgeon. Both of David's parents were also martyred in Viet Nam, where they had spent twenty years as missionaries. Undaunted, David and Becki set about establishing the famous Bongolo CMA Mission Hospital in Gabon, West Africa, which now serves one-third of the entire country. Thousands of people have accepted Jesus Christ as Savior and many thousands have been healed. As a prisoner of hope, the Lord has "restored double" to Betty Mitchell.

Most of us will not experience martyrdom as the Apostle Paul, Archie Mitchell and the Thompsons did. But when we face problems that weigh us down, may we bear in mind that we, as prisoners of the Lord are prisoners "to a living hope through the resurrection of Jesus Christ from the dead, to an inheritance incorruptible and undefiled and that does not fade away, reserved in Heaven for you" (1 Peter 1:3-4).

"Now may the God of hope fill you with all joy and peace in believing, that you may abide in hope by the power of the Holy Spirit" (Romans 15:13). Dr. Roger Hinrichs, Professor of Nuclear Physics, notes: "God's love is not always found in our circumstances, but God's love is always found in our hope."

Purpose and Plans

"Everyone who is called by My name, whom I have created for My glory; I have formed him, yes, I have made him."

(Isaiah 43:7)

"God has a plan for your life." Have you ever been told that? We often proffer this truth to someone who has lost hope in an effort to inspire in him or her a desire to learn more about God or to introduce Him to someone who is considering the way of salvation. The God of Israel made this promise to His people who were then in Babylon, having been exiled from Jerusalem at about 600 B.C. He was assuring them that after seventy years of captivity, His plans were to restore them. "For I know the thoughts that I think toward you, thoughts of peace and not of evil, to give you a future and a hope" (Jeremiah 29:11). The word "thoughts" in this case alludes to the idea of a "plan" for their lives. So, while it is a fact that God has plans for "peace and the good life" for each of His children, there is a much deeper truth we need to uncover. God has an underlying "purpose" for each of us and His plans stem from and grow out of that "purpose."

A plan is one thing; a purpose is quite another. Purpose is that entity that forms the groundwork—is the basis for—a plan. Without a purpose, a plan would be useless. "In Him we have redemption through His blood, the forgiveness of sins, according to the riches of His grace which He made to abound toward us in all wisdom and prudence (insight), having made known to us the mystery of His will, according to His good pleasure which He *purposed* in Himself" (Ephesians 1:7-9 emphasis added). "In Him also we have obtained an inheritance, being predestined according to the *purpose* of Him who works all things according to the counsel of His will, that we who first trusted in Christ should be to the praise of His glory" (Ephesians 1:11-12 emphasis added). Simply stated yet with the complexity of the ages, God tells us that His eternal "purpose" was accomplished through Christ Jesus our Lord (see Ephesians 3:11).

His purpose for those of us who first trusted in Christ is that we should live to glorify Him—flesh out the proper estimation of Him—to the world, as Paul reminds us in Ephesians 1:11. This is also borne out in Isaiah 43:7 as the Old Testament prophet spoke of the Redeemer to Israel and to future generations as well. "Everyone who is called by My name, whom

I have created for My glory, I have formed him, yes, I have made him." 2 Timothy 1:9 sums up God's purpose nicely for each of us, "(God) has saved us and called us with a holy calling, not according to our works, but according to His own *purpose* and grace which was given us in Christ Jesus before time began" (emphasis added).

Dr. Adrian Rogers tells a story of a young boy named Bobby, whose father usually brought a gift for him when he returned from his travels. He was disappointed when his Dad came home this time without one. His father promised the son that they would go shopping the next day and the boy could buy anything he wanted—anything.

First, they came upon some of the child's favorite candy and the boy said, "This is what I want."

"Don't you think we had better look a little farther to see if there is something you would like better?" asked his father.

As they approached the toy department they spotted a red, white and blue kite exactly like the one Bobby had said he wanted, but his father urged him to keep on looking. As they passed by a display of shoes, sure enough there were the very same cowboy boots that the boy had admired in the store window.

"We can come back," said his Dad, "if you don't find something you like better."

Becoming weary, they finally arrived at the back of the store, where stood the best looking silver and red Mongoose bicycle that either of them had ever seen.

Wide eyed, the lad asked, "You really mean I can have that bike?" as he leaped for joy.

"That is what I had planned for you all along, Son," replied his Dad.

As you've already concluded, the boy's father wanted to give him the very best and he wanted his boy to realize that.

So it is with our Heavenly Father. We must place our faith and hope in His plans for us, for it is His purpose—His pleasure—to give us that which is the very best for us—eternal life.

"And we know that all things work together for good to those who love God, to those who are the called according to His *purpose*." (Romans 8:28)

Removing the Grave-clothes

✥

"Bear one another's burdens, and so fulfill the law of Christ." (Galatians 6:2)

R emoving the grave-clothes and bearing one another's burdens are essentially the same thing. Of the seven miracles recorded in the Gospel of John, perhaps the resurrection of Lazarus from the grave (the seventh) is the most extra-ordinary (see John 11:1-44). Lazarus (whose name means "God is helper" or "God of help"), had been dead four days. He was interred in a tomb with a stone protecting the entrance, according to the custom in Jesus' time. Jesus cried loudly, "'Lazarus, come forth!' and he who had died came bound hand and foot with grave-clothes, and his face was wrapped with a cloth" (John 11:43-44). Engaging the help of those standing by, Jesus said to them, "Loose him and let him go." They complied and Lazarus was delivered from the confines and stench that a four-day period of death and burial had affected. Jesus, who made all things, calmed the storm at sea, and walked on water, did not *need* assistance from people to free Lazarus. Yet, He *chose* to enlist the help of people in removing this man's grave-clothes, the final step in loosing him from bondage.

Jesus has set forth a prototype for us to contemplate in this narration. It is not a parable; rather, it is the historical account of one man's encounter with death and renewed life. Most of us will not be counted a statistic among those who have ostensibly died and miraculously been brought back to life. There will be times however, when we find ourselves *bound* by circumstances in which there seems to be no way out. Jesus assures us that others have faced the same problem. He has made "a way of escape" for them and He promises to do the same for us (see 1 Corinthians 10:13).

In his book, "The Purpose Driven Life," Rick Warren observes that there are over fifty times in the New Testament where the phrase "one another" or "each other" is used in conjunction with "pray for, encourage, admonish, serve, teach, submit, and bear one another's burdens." Burdens dealing with divorce, drug abuse, death of a loved one, loss of a job, or an accident that has brought on suffering seems to cry out for a soft shoulder to lean upon. We generally seek someone who has *been there or been through it* and understands; whether it is a disability or worse yet, death.

Recovery from addictions or any other form of backsliding, need not—should not—be borne alone. "Let the word of Christ richly dwell within you, with all wisdom teaching and admonishing *one another* with psalms and hymns and spiritual songs, singing with thankfulness in your hearts to God" (Colossians 3:16 NIV emphasis added). "Therefore comfort *each other* and edify *one another*, just as you also are doing" (1 Thessalonians 5:11 emphasis added). "Wherefore comfort yourselves *together*, and edify *one another*, even as also ye do" (1 Thessalonians 5:11 KJV emphasis added).

Sharing our burdens makes us less vulnerable to one of the devil's favorite weapons—discouragement. "Exhort *one another* daily, as long as it is called 'Today,' lest any of you be hardened by the deceitfulness of sin" (Hebrews 3:13 emphasis added).

The Apostle Paul's desire was "…that I may be encouraged together with you by the mutual faith both of you and me" (Romans 1:12). During those times when our faith seems too weak to endure, the faith of others, that "mutual faith" will bear us up. Your faith helps my faith and vice versa. A friend doesn't always need advice during the tough times. It may be that going out for breakfast together once a week or just "hanging out" for a couple of hours is all that is needed to succor a wounded spirit. It may require offering a sympathetic, listening ear and a kind helping hand for weeks on end. All of this must be couched in agape love, God's love and prayer.

We may be called upon to "remove the grave-clothes"—help "loose" that one who is hopelessly bound in a web of circumstance. Bear in mind that Jesus is the Healer, Jehovah Rapha. Our part is to *be there* to help so that he or she may be "loosed"—set free to experience new life. It is not our ability, but our *availability* that counts. "Confess your trespasses to *one another,* and pray for *one another,* that you may be healed. The effective, fervent prayer of a righteous man avails much" (James 5:16 emphasis added).

"And above all things have fervent love for *one another*, for love will cover a multitude of sins." (1 Peter 4:8 emphasis added)

Resurrection Power

"I say to you, unless a grain of wheat falls into the ground and dies, it remains alone; but if it dies, it produces much grain." (John 12:24)

There are eight recorded occasions in Scripture where people were actually resurrected apart from the greatest account of all, that of the Lord Jesus Christ. Old Testament prophets Elijah and Elisha each raised a boy from the dead and Elisha's bones restored a man to life (see 1 Kings 17:22 and 2 Kings 4:34-35). Jesus revived a widow's son from Nain in Luke 7:14-15 and Jairus' daughter in Luke 8:52-56. Lazarus was made alive again after being dead four days in John 11:38-44. Peter restored Dorcas, that woman who was "full of good works and charitable deeds," to life in Acts 9:40-41. Paul raised up Eutychus, a young man who fell to his death out of a third story window in Acts 20:7-12. These are supernatural accounts of resurrection, but we realize that in each case, those raised eventually died again.

Jesus Christ is the exception—He was God's only begotten Son. He was born in a manger, He increased in wisdom and in stature (Luke 2:52); lived about thirty-three years; died a cruel death on the cross for man's sin (Matthew 27:32-55); and was destined to rise on the third day (Matthew 28:1-7); never to die again. As Mediator, He is now seated at the right hand of God the Father, where He *ever* lives to make intercession for those of us who belong to Him (Hebrews l2:2; 7:25). He is alive forevermore.

We take for granted such illustrations of *resurrection power* as the flowers of spring when they bravely thrust tiny new heads up through the crust of earth under which they were buried; or a butterfly as it emerges from a cocoon; or a new life that emerges from a grain of wheat that has died; or the rainbow of promise God sends to remind us of the new life available to us even after a flood. But there remains a more personal facet of this "energy," of this resurrection power that we can *know* experientially. The Apostle Paul prayed that, "the eyes of your understanding being enlightened; that you may know what is the hope of His calling, what are the riches of the glory of His inheritance in the saints, and what is the exceeding greatness of His mighty power *toward us who believe*, according to the working of His mighty power which He worked in Christ when He raised Him from the dead and seated Him at His right hand in the heavenly places" (Ephesians 1:18-20). He passionately wanted all believers to be aware of the magnitude of God's provision for us.

When was the last time that you were pressed beyond measure—overwhelmed with what lay ahead, but after turning to God in prayer, received strength to complete the task? Looking back, do you find that you almost "breezed" through the ordeal once you invited God into the situation? What of the pastor who is all ready to deliver a zealous message of encouragement to his flock when, shortly before church time, he receives word of a dire family tragedy? Where can he turn but to God who will enable him to minister in the power of the Spirit? Anyone who has been stricken with a serious illness—or perhaps just a common cold or the "flu"—upon recovering, will attest to the healing powers that God has infused into our bodies which are so "fearfully and wonderfully made" (Psalm 139:14).

While I was in India some years ago undergoing tremendous emotional and physical stress, an elder-mentor-friend arranged for me to witness to approximately seventy-five women at an Assembly called Hebron. When I asked to be relieved of the commitment, he replied that God had a message for these people at this time and I was merely the instrument to deliver it. He was right. Though I remained in what seemed like a haze and could barely remember what was presented, God used His mighty word (translated into Telegu) to encourage and edify. This was a definite encounter with His *resurrection power.* Possibly without realizing it, you have experienced a brush of it also.

C.S. Lewis, author of The Chronicles of Narnia, originally professed to be an atheist. After his conversion to Christianity he became one of the most provocative teachers, authors, and theologians of the twentieth century. Lewis said, "The world is crowded with God," implying that we could and should be aware of His presence wherever we are. Similarly, the world is crowded with glimpses of His *resurrection power* but it often passes by unobserved. We will never experience the fullness of it until that day when we shall be caught up to meet the Lord in the air, to be with Him always (see 1Thessalonians 4:l7). As we wait for that expectant hope, let's focus on the present and be encouraged by those times when God restores or renews our energy, visiting us with a touch of His *resurrection* power.

"Now to Him that is able to do exceedingly abundantly above all that we ask or think, according to the **power** that works in us, to Him be glory in the church by Christ Jesus to all generations, forever and ever. Amen."

(Ephesians 3:20)

Safeguarded by God's Causes

❖

"'You shall know that I have done nothing without *cause* that I have done,' says the Lord God." (Ezekiel 14:23)

Life is a series of events or episodes encased in God-ordained parentheses. You may be sitting on top of the world; enjoying good health, a lovely family, the job of your choice, and looking towards a brilliant future. Praise the Lord. It's possible, however, that you are bearing a burden, a weight, a heavy cross or whatever your thorn may be. Praise the Lord anyhow! It is not without cause that you are where you are; it is to draw *someone* closer to the Lord; if not you, perhaps someone you love very much. And you can be sure that God will *cause* it to work together for your good. You are hedged in—you are living in between and you are protected by at least two of God's *causes.*

The prophet Ezekiel was chosen by God to deliver a most unwelcome message in the early chapters of his book; that of the impending destruction of the city of Jerusalem. It was a doomsday message. The house of Israel had been consistently unfaithful and now the time had come for God to deal with their disobedience. Not only had this happened before, but history confirms that it would be repeated time and again. Human nature hasn't changed a bit in the past 2500 years. The cycle is prophetic. Nations made up of people like you and I continue to deliberately sin; God chastens us; we repent; God blesses. Romans 15:4 tells us, "Everything that was written in the past was written to teach us, so that through endurance and the encouragement of the Scriptures, we might have hope" (NIV).

God has painted a vivid word picture for us in Ezekiel 14:12-23. The Lord God encouraged His prophet saying if He were to send a famine to the land or a sword or pestilence or cause wild beasts to roam about rendering desolation, people like Noah, Daniel, and Job would still survive. Nations may devise diabolical schemes to glorify man rather than God, but there will always be a few righteous people, a remnant, to justify our hope. After we, as individuals, have strayed from God's counsel, our only recourse is to retrace our steps (physically or spiritually or both) back to the place where we began to waver. We must reap the consequences of our sins. "Do not be deceived, God is not mocked; for whatever a man sows, that he will also reap" (Galatians 6:7). However, if we repent,

He will cause that *episode* to work together for our good, according to Romans 8:28. "And we know that God *causes* all things to work together for good to those who love God, to those who are the called, according to His purpose" (NAS). Once we seek forgiveness, we are ready to do business with God.

Whether we are living with feast or famine, getting an education, making a vital decision, raising a family, experiencing empty nest syndrome, battling sickness, or making plans for retirement, remember that episode didn't come to stay—it will pass. Our lives are evolving within a series of parenthesis safeguarded on both ends by God's *causes*.

Salt of the Earth

✤

"You are the salt of the earth; but if the salt loses its flavor, how shall it be seasoned? It is then good for nothing, but to be thrown out and trampled under foot by men."

(Matthew 5:13)

W hy did God label those who follow Him, "the salt of the earth"? Our first clue is found in Leviticus 2:13. The Israelites are a free people once again having been delivered from Egypt. They have arrived safely at the foot of Mt. Sinai and the tabernacle has been completed. The Lord speaks to Moses giving His people specific instructions for their offerings, of which there would be five specific categories.

"And every offering of your grain offering you shall season with *salt*; you shall not allow the *salt* of the covenant of your God to be lacking from your grain offering. With all your offerings you shall offer *salt*" (Leviticus 2:13). This was one of the holy covenants in Bible times. It was also called the "salt of the covenant" because as men confirmed their covenants with each other by eating and drinking together, salt was *always* used. There was a "chamber of salt" in the temple reserved especially for this purpose. Not only was salt a holy symbol pertaining to sacrifice offerings, it was also a covenant of friendship and loyalty.

Another example of "covenant" regarding holy things was the offerings for priests and Levites. The Lord vowed to Aaron, "All the heave offerings of the holy things, which the children of Israel offer to the Lord, I have given to you and your sons and daughters with you as an ordinance forever; it is a covenant of *salt* forever before the Lord with you and your descendants with you" (Numbers 18:19). It appears that salt, with its power to enhance flavor and keep food from decay, would symbolize some sort of unbending truthfulness such as would be expected in surrendering ourselves to the Lord. It was a vital part of "covenant" in those days. In 2 Chronicles 13:5 we learn that God gave the kingdom of Israel over to David and his sons forever, by a covenant of salt. Ezekiel tells us that after the sacrificed animals had been ceremonially cleansed, they would be offered to the Lord, but not until the priests had cast *salt* upon them (see Ezekiel 43:13-24).

Apart from its covenant use, salt had monetary value also. Years ago, it was vital to the economy and was used as a substitute for money. Wages and salaries were paid in salt.

The word "salary" is derived from the Latin "salari(um)" or "salt money." A lazy man may be referred to as "a man who is not worth his salt."

Salt also has healing power. Old Testament prophet Elijah was taken up by a whirlwind into heaven, and a chariot of fire parted him and his successor, Elisha, at the river Jordan according to 2 Kings 2:9-12. The water was bad, making the land unfruitful. "Bring me a new bowl and put salt in it," said Elisha. Then he threw the salt into the waters and said, "I have healed these waters…so the water remains healed to this day" (2 Kings 2:20-22). Anyone who has suffered with a sore throat and has gargled with salt water knows that salt heals. In Bible times, travel routes were often based on locations of salt deposits.

Cultures and cities with large deposits thrived. A more recent example is the city of Syracuse—a large community in Central New York, built during the 18th and 19th centuries and founded on salt. Historically, it became known as "Salt City." Even today, its identity is confirmed by the Salt City Playhouse; Salt City Soccer; Salt Museum, etc. Salt potatoes were "birthed" here. As miners came to work, they would place their lunches—usually potatoes—in storage vats until lunch time. Through the process of osmosis, enough salt would be absorbed to make for a zesty meal. Thus, people from all over the country have come to enjoy Central New York's "salt potatoes."

Marriage covenants are sometimes solemnized by a "salt ceremony" rather than the typical candle lighting service. Salt is used because it is a type of the church as in Matthew 5:13. The bride and groom each bring a small container (usually a pouch) of salt to the altar. They pour their separate portions into one small vessel which is then shaken vigorously. The only way this "contract" can be broken is for each one to retrieve his/her own grains of salt, which is virtually impossible. The symbolism is powerful! Figuratively, bride and groom become one inseparable unit.

"Salt is good, but if the salt loses its flavor, how will you season it? Have salt in yourselves, have peace with one another" (Mark 9:50). We are valuable in God's economy. He expects us, His children, to live sacrificial lives, showing forth the propensities of salt. It flavors—makes God's Word palatable; it preserves—slows down decay (of society); it defrosts—melts ice (icy hearts); and heals through cleansing (wounded lives). Let's make sure that we have salt in ourselves and sprinkle a little of that salt over our relationships with others so that as God's witnesses, our testimony will appeal to them.

"Let your *speech* always be with grace, seasoned with salt, that you may know how you ought to answer each one." (Colossians 4:6)

Servant—Friend

✤

"You are my friends if you do whatever I command you. No longer do I call you servants, for a servant does not know what his master is doing; but I have called you friends, for all things that I heard from My Father I have made known to you." (John 15:14-15)

"Mrs. B. feeds her servants and treats them well," remarked my missionary friend, as we observed the small sari-draped figure scurrying toward home at twilight. She was carrying a covered bucket which left a pungent, unmistakable aroma of curried rice in its wake. My friend's reference was to a neighbor lady, an Indian matron whose reputation for kindness toward her maidservants was obviously well established in that part of Southern India.

Robbery being almost routine there, it is the responsibility of the mistress of a home to place under lock and key any valuables belonging to her family until the hireling leaves. Laws governing thievery are seldom enforced due to the *volume* of crimes committed in this heavily populated land. The relationship between this mistress and her domestic, however, had obviously taken on a flavor that defies the commonplace. Jesus describes it this way in John 15:15, "No longer do I call you servants, for a servant does not know what his master is doing; but I have called you friends, for all things that I heard from My Father I have made known to you."

As a rule, a servant serves because he *has* to, a hireling serves because he *needs* to, and a brother serves because he *ought* to, but a friend serves because he *wants* to. Jesus calls us friends if we do whatever He commands us, explaining that we are no longer "in the dark" about what He is doing, as a servant would be. Abraham was called the friend of God according to James 2:23. God made a covenant with Abraham, outlining specific details as to his progeny; defining his future for his ears alone. "My covenant is with you, and you shall be a father of many nations" (Genesis 17:4). By the same token, God will reveal His plans for us in His time. He is our Friend, the sort of friend who would lay down His life for us. He did just that while we were yet sinners who couldn't have cared less at the time (see Romans 5:8).

While nothing could compensate for the gift of eternal life which Jesus Christ gave to us, it is fitting, it is our privilege, and our high calling to serve Him. However, if we give or serve out of compulsion rather than motivated by our love for Him, we forfeit gladness and joy. The Salvation Army, a Christian International Organization founded in England in 1865, devoted its purpose to impart life to the poor and needy through evangelistic outreach and social services. Their motto has remained, "Saved to Serve." God is bound to be glorified in the process.

Mrs. B. bequeaths clothes her children outgrow (there are no thrift shops in India); colorful new outfits at Christmas time and food from her table to her servants. It is done with a light heart. How God loves a cheerful giver! When a servant becomes a friend, the door to our heart is open and we can throw away the key.

When Jesus said, "No longer do I call you servants, but I have called you friends," He did not exclude the Master-servant relationship. Indeed, He made it more precious.

Seven Last Sayings of Christ

✤

"Father, forgive them for they do not know what they do"

(Luke 23:34).

In Jesus' first response from the Cross of Calvary, He fulfilled a prophecy that Isaiah had made approximately 700 years earlier (Isaiah 53:12). The entire 53rd Chapter of Isaiah presents a graphic account of the life and death of Jesus Christ. Old Testament saints looked forward to the Messiah, just as we look back to His crucifixion. The resurrection of Jesus Christ gives us the glorious hope and assurance of an eternal heavenly home.

"Assuredly, I say to you, today you will be with Me in paradise" (Luke 23:43). Jesus encouraged the thief on the cross. It was for this purpose that He was willing to suffer, so that the thief and you and I might be with Him in paradise.

"Woman, behold your son!" Then He said to His disciple, "Behold your mother" (John 19:26-27). John, the disciple "whom Jesus loved," was the only male follower there at the cross. Jesus' mother, His mother's sister, Mary the wife of Clopas, and Mary Magdalene were also there. Jesus encouraged his mother to consider John as her son from then on and vice versa. "From that hour that disciple took her into his own home." (See John 19:27).

"And about the ninth hour, Jesus cried with a loud voice, saying, 'Eli, Eli, lama sabachthani?' that is, *'My God, My God, why have you forsaken me?*" (Matthew 27:46). In verse 45 Matthew tells us, "Now from the sixth hour until the ninth hour there was darkness over all the land." According to our reckoning of time, this would have been from Noon to 3:00 P.M. Jesus literally took all of our sins on Himself and the sins of all those who would eventually accept Him as Savior.

"After this, Jesus, knowing that all things were now accomplished, that the Scripture might be fulfilled, said, 'I thirst'" (John 19:28). Thus, another Messianic prophecy, written hundreds of years previously, was fulfilled. We read in Psalm 69:20-2, "Reproach has broken my heart, and I am full of heaviness; I looked for someone to take pity, but there was none; and for comforters, but I found none. They also gave me gall for my food, and for my thirst they gave me vinegar to drink." Jesus received vinegar or sour wine rather than water as He hung on the cross.

"It is finished" (John 19:30). The word "finished" here represents a bookkeeping term meaning "paid in full." Jesus had completed the purpose for which He had come to earth. Just before this, He had prayed probably the most powerful supplication of all time, as revealed in John 17:1-26. "I have glorified You on earth. I have finished the work which You have given Me to do. And now, O Father, glorify Me together with Yourself, with the glory which I had with You before the world was" (John 17:4-5). That "work" encompassed the defeat of satan and death. There is no more the "sting" of death for the believer. Satan lost the battle for souls, except for those who will not accept Christ's gift of redemption through the blood He shed on Calvary's tree. Soon after His burial, Jesus would reappear in His resurrected body, offering not only salvation but immortality to every believer.

"He said, 'Father, into Your hands I commit My spirit.' Having said this, He breathed His last" (Luke 23:46). "And bowing His head, He gave up His Spirit" (John 19:30b). These were Jesus' very last words as He hung on the cross. The anguish that we detected when He prayed, "My God, My God, why have You forsaken Me?" (Matthew 27:46) has been replaced with a quiet, calm spirit. Again, He addresses God as "Father." The darkness is over. History tells us that it often took six days for a victim of crucifixion to die. However, Jesus died in approximately six hours, His death fulfilling over 300

Biblical prophecies. Soldiers came to break the prisoners' legs as was the custom, but because He had already died, Jesus' legs were not broken (Psalm 34:20). "Then they will look on Me whom they pierced" (Zechariah 12:10).

"For God so loved the world that He gave His only begotten son, that whoever believes in Him should not perish, but have everlasting life" (John 3:16).

"He is risen from the dead" (Matt.28:7) and He is alive forevermore!

ShadowsShadows

✤

"Yea, though I walk through the valley of the shadow of death, I will fear no evil." (Psalm 23:4)

A small shrill voice pierced the late night stillness: "Daddy! Come quickly! Something's moving in my room!"

Daddy bounded up the stairs and enveloped the little boy in his "father bear" arms. Moonlit shadows were playing tag on the curtains. With a flick of the light switch, all the lad's fears were gone—the shadows having been chased away by the lighted lamp near his bed.

The Old Testament Book of Job uses the phrase "shadow of death" ten times. First, it appears in Job 3:4-5 as Job curses the day he was born saying, "May God above not seek it, nor the light shine upon it. May darkness and the shadow of death claim it." He indicates that darkness and the shadow of death are synonymous. But are they? In Job 10:21-22, still deploring his birth, he speaks of returning to the "land of darkness and the shadow of death…without any order, where even the light is darkness." Having experienced tremendous loss, his emotions have understandably taken control of his senses. Have you ever entertained thoughts like these while in the throes of depression? Fortunately, this is not a true picture of death for God's people.

The "shadow of death" appears over fifteen times in Scripture. The Psalmist speaks of "those who sat in darkness and in the shadow of death" (Psalm 107:10). Then Psalm 107:14 tells us, "He brought them out of darkness and the shadow of death." Jeremiah refers to Israel's delivery from Egyptian captivity in Jeremiah 2:6, "…the Lord, who brought us up out of the land of Egypt, who led us through the wilderness, through a land of deserts and pits…of drought and the shadow of death." We read in Jeremiah 13:16, "Give glory to the Lord your God before He causes darkness and before your feet stumble…and while you are looking for light, He turns it into the shadow of death." We find in Amos 5:8 that the Lord "turns the shadow of death into morning," the idea being that light displaces the shadow. Shadows occur specifically when something obscures the light. Shadows scare us because evil hides in darkness.

However, the only reference to the "valley" of the shadow of death is made by King David in the 23rd Psalm. Life's valleys are often threatening but the Lord is God of the valleys as well as God of the hills. It is in the darkness of the valley where many dear souls have gone through almost unbearable ordeals of extreme physical and mental suffering, causing them to cry out for deliverance. Each person's journey through the "valley of life" is unique to him. Our deliverance from the valley of pain and its accompanying fear lies in the resurrection of Jesus Christ, the Light of the world (John 8:12). The believer's hope lies in Jesus Christ, the Light at the end of the tunnel. When we cross over into the New Jerusalem, our Heavenly Home, the Lamb is its light and it is illuminated by the glory of God (see Revelation 21:22-23). With the shadow of death behind us, we shall realize that our fears were groundless.

Nowhere in God's Word do we find a reference to death as annihilation or cessation of existence. In John 11:9-14 Jesus explains to the mourners that Lazarus "slept" when he was actually dead. We learn from the text that after four days of death (sleep) in the tomb, Jesus performed the miracle of Lazarus' resurrection, after which He declared, "I am the resurrection and the life." Thereby assuring us there is life after death.

We often hear the expression "beyond the shadow of a doubt." In his book *Disciplines of the Inner Life*, Robert Benson declared: "Doubt is the shadow caused by faith." Have you ever entertained a doubt? Probably everyone has. Our faith is the result of our belief in Jesus Christ, the Light of the world. Doubt, therefore, would cast a shadow on that faith. Without some semblance of enlightened faith, a doubt would never occur. Science confirms what we can plainly see: a shadow is caused by a light much larger than itself. The sun and moon are our best illustration of reflected light. The moon has no light of itself; it is strictly a reflection of the sun. Yet moonlight is as much a part of our sky as sunlight. It brightens up our night sky with wondrous beauty, although the sun is its source. Christians, who were living in darkness having no light of their own, ought to reflect Jesus Christ, the Light of the world. Shadows themselves are fleeting, harmless; in fact, they are not real at all. Just as the light in the little boy's room superseded those shadows on his wall, so the light of the Lamb cancels out death's shadow for all eternity.

"So when this corruptible has put on incorruption, and this mortal has put on immortality, then shall be brought to pass the saying that is written: 'Death is swallowed up in victory.' " (1 Corinthians 15:54)

Shadows

Shadows merry, leaping, dancing,
Lending shade from noonday sun;
Twilight shadows peeping, prancing,

Bending leaf and branch as one;

Nighttime shadows scale the trellis,

Creeping, crawling on the wall;

Morning light returns to tell us-

Shadows are not real at all.

-Natalie Pierce

Shelter in the Time of Storm

✤

"I would hasten my escape from the windy storm and tempest." (Psalm 55:8)

D uring this past winter, we endured a record number of frigid days and snowfall. Then, as if for a grand finale, April brought with it a great ice storm which left in its wake broken buildings, downed electric and telephone wires, and perhaps most discouraging of all, countless broken shattered trees, some representing 100 or 200 years of growth. Our mind's eye pictures *"what was"* as we gaze at *"what is,"* and we are saddened by the loss. We stood helplessly by and watched ice laden branches and huge trees—mighty oaks and maples—bow, bend and break—capitulating to the merciless ice storm as it pelted the earth.

Their more fragile counterparts, the willows and birches, suffered the greater damage. Most of them were left with their tops bending dejectedly to the ground, unable to bear the weight of several inches of ice. As though struck by lightning, many of them were rent from top to bottom, their beauty and function now banished to the woodpile. Even some of the more robust trees fell as martyrs. That is bad news, but the good news is that the storms fury acted as a catharsis, pruning and purging as it cleaned out the weaker, unhealthy trees, while simultaneously clearing space for fresh, new growth. Storms serve to weaken the weak and strengthen the strong.

Storm shelters were set up to assist those people who were without heat and light as a result of electric cables that had snapped under the burden of ice. Churches, government buildings, and schools were quickly and efficiently converted to living quarters where folks were encouraged to take refuge. Friends, families and neighbors shared their homes and apartments with those less fortunate until power was restored. Candles and flashlights cast an eerie glow within shelters and homes. At our house, we had a prolonged "slumber party," where everyone slept cozily on the living room floor, warmed with heat from the fireplace.

A most unique *shelter* was "arranged" despite the biting cold, just under the overhang of our garage. Several days previous to the storm, a pair of Phoebe birds (members of the flycatcher family) had elected to set up housekeeping there. These little birds have scissor-like tails that swish back and forth incessantly and they repeatedly sing a cheery, "fee-bee, fee-bee." Their nest building began with mud "pasted" against the house, supported by a small wire, to which they had added twigs for stability and leaves for comfort. During the storm, tumbling trees and branches had shaken the very rafters of our house. Even the garage roof was "fractured" here and there, especially around the eaves.

The last thing that I expected to survive was the little birds' nest. It was within a few inches of the *damaged* roof. But the morning after the storm, I was riveted to the spot when outside my window sounded, "fee-bee, fee-bee." There were the Phoebes—safe and secure—in their small haven. Isn't it just like God to do that? Why should we be surprised? Didn't He say that although "the birds of the air neither sow nor reap" (Matthew 6:26) He cares for them? He had outfitted those tiny creatures of song with *a shelter in the time of storm.*

Our home on the river was surrounded by dozens of trees, old and young, creating a miniature woodland reminiscent of the Adirondack mountains. Many of those trees were on the casualty list of this mighty storm. For two days we held our breath, while huge branches creaked, snapped, descended on and then slid off our rooftop. We were thankful that no one was injured.

Psalm 61:3-4 took on new meaning for us: "For You have been a shelter for me, a strong tower from the enemy, I will abide in Your tabernacle forever; I will trust in the shelter of Your wings." God is *our shelter in the time of storm* also.

Shut In - Not Shut Out

❖

"For as we have many members in one body, and all members do not have the same function; so we, being many, are one body in Christ, and individually members one of another." (Romans 12:4-5)

Patients in our local nursing home sat at attention, those who could sit either in chairs or wheelchairs, while others had been brought in on their beds. They all gathered around a long table, which was piled high with Large Print Bibles and books containing hymns and choruses. Light hearted jokes and chatter filled our meeting room, as the staff cheerfully wheeled in one patient after another. We averaged ten to fifteen people each week.

Andy, a pharmacist/teacher paraplegic victim of MS, encouraged us with his ready wit and a remedy for almost any ailment. Carl, who had cerebral palsy, flashed a contagious smile each time he asked us to sing his favorite hymn,

"The Old Rugged Cross." Irene, a former teacher stroke patient, had adjusted with grace and humility to her new life in a wheelchair. She was a charmer who became our point of reference for history and grammar. Bessie, a saucy little old lady whose musical prowess had won her much acclaim in bygone days, enhanced our song time as her gnarled fingers found the piano keys. Bessie had "heart" and everybody loved to hear her play.

My mother had been a patient at this facility and whenever my sister, Norma and I were with her, we read Scripture and prayed together. Others noticed our daily visits and began asking questions.

One bright eyed eighty year old lady asked, "Could you tell me where the Bible says, 'they shall mount up with wings as eagles?' "

We pointed her to Isaiah 40:3l. The idea caught on quickly as others joined in with further queries, some out of curiosity and some with purer motives. Eventually, their diverse interests spawned a genuine zeal, as the Holy Spirit began speaking to these dear souls.

One day our Mom suffered a stroke from which she never recovered. The Lord took her home. Some time later, still grieving deeply, my sister and I stopped by the nursing home to comfort our new found friends. We were "swamped" with requests to continue the Bible Studies. After much prayer, we approached the administrator of the institution, apprising him of the situation. His response was gratifying. He offered to reserve the lounge on a weekly basis where we could encourage men and women to come for a time of worship, prayer, study and fellowship.

God was already at work. It was our privilege to join Him in what proved to be several years of getting to know God and each other at a deeper level. We became a people whose hearts were knit together with threads of sorrow and pain; gladness and joy. Although these nursing home residents were shut in, they were no longer shut out from God's comfort and counsel.

Shut In - Not Shut Out – Part 2

❖

"...But as his part is who goes down to the battle, so shall his part be who stays by the supplies; they shall share alike." (I Samuel 30:24)

The Bible, good news to all of us, carries a special message of hope to shut-ins. The Amalakites, David's arch enemies who had pilfered all their lives, killing for the sheer pleasure of doing so, had burned the city of Ziklag, and taken captive the wives, sons and daughters of David and his men. Not only was David's family imprisoned by the enemy, but his people were threatening to stone him. At this crucial point, we read, "...David strengthened himself in the Lord his God" (I Samuel 30:6).When we reach rock bottom, the only way to restore our perspective is to encourage ourselves in the Lord our God. After David received instruction from the Lord, he set out with 600 men to "recap" their losses. Of the 600 men chosen, 200 were so faint that they were forced to remain behind. When the battle was over, "David recovered all" (1 Samuel 30:19). Some of the warriors objected to the spoils being evenly divided. They argued that the 200 men who were left behind should receive a lesser portion. David's judgment was: "But as his part is who goes down to the battle, so shall his part be who stays (stands) by the supplies; they shall share alike. So it was, from that day forward; he made it a statute and an ordinance for Israel to this day" (I Samuel 30:24-25).

God set up a standard and the pattern established at that time remains in effect today. What a hope for the infirm; a promise for those who languish on beds of pain; for those who are confined and shut-in. Many who are too weary and faint to enter the foray—the front lines—have become powerful prayer warriors, interceding for friends, family, and missionaries far afield. Some of these dear ones offer a sympathetic, listening ear to others who are hurting. Since they no longer circulate in the crowd, their priorities have changed. One health care facility resident, a Christian lady, has a delightful ministry of knitting mittens for needy children. She is a real spirit-lifter. Blooming where they are planted, these believers are "standing by the stuff."

A Christian soldier may march into battle or assume a position behind the lines, as God directs. No matter, the prospect is exciting! The share of those who stay behind is to be the same as that of those who go down to the battle. All will share alike. God said so. Shut-ins are not shut-out!

Something Missing

"In everything by prayer and supplication with thanksgiving let your requests be made known unto God. And the peace of God, which passeth all understanding, shall keep your hearts and minds through Christ Jesus."

(Philippians 4:6,7 KJV)

D an, a young college student, phoned his grandmother in a distant city asking her to pray for his fiancée. She had graduated from a prestigious university, gone on to graduate school, and now she was ready to take a very important exam. Whether she passed or not would most likely determine the course of her future. Immediately following a time of prayer, Dan breathed a sigh of relief. "Thanks, Gram, I knew there was *something missing*." Without prayer, we are also likely to find *something missing* from our crowded agendas. How many times in the recent past have we found ourselves in a similar situation? Incidentally, Shelley did pass the exam.

It was a mild evening in Virginia and the stores were jammed with Christmas shoppers at the mall. A young woman named Crystal finished shopping, got in her car and as she fastened the seat belt, noticed that an earring was missing—it had fallen off. It was her favorite pair—ruby studded, 22K gold, and although quite expensive, her main concern was that they had come from India, her native land. They were irreplaceable. After a fruitless search of the store where clerks kindly assisted her in retracing her steps, they scanned the parking lot also, but to no avail. About three hours later, at home and feeling a bit dejected, it "dawned" on her that she had never really prayed about it. So she offered up what Catherine Marshall called a "prayer of relinquishment."

"Lord, I know that there are more important concerns in life than this piece of jewelry. I leave the situation in Your capable Hands. If You had wanted me to find that earring, I would have found it. So I give it up to You."

Suddenly, she felt the urge to return to the mall. It was late, but in the poorly lit parking lot she re-searched the area where the car had been parked. Lo and behold! There on the yellow divider line was a tiny ruby earring—intact—twinkling up at her.

Her spirit soared! Not because of the restored gem; (that was secondary now), but because she had realized that there was *something missing*, remembered her first priority—

prayer, and God answered immediately. We are aware that God does not always answer our prayers so directly. But we know that He <u>does</u> answer every one of them: "Yes," "No," or "Wait." He *entreats* us: "Call unto Me, and I will answer you, and show thee great and mighty things, which you do not know" (Jeremiah 33:3).

Such direct access to our Heavenly Father rests on the fact that when Mary, Mary Magdalene and the other women went to Jesus' tomb bringing spices with which to anoint Him, they found *something missing*—the body of Jesus. He was no longer there. He *is* no longer there. The tomb is empty! He was crucified for our sins, died, and was buried. But now He is *risen* and seated at the right hand of the throne of God. Jesus, the author and finisher of our faith, has paved the way for us! We come before Him with our supplications and thanksgiving, based on a personal relationship with Jesus Christ. Perhaps then, we should resolve to take every advantage of the privilege that prayer offers. If we make it a high priority to pray *first*, we will avoid the consequences of *something missing*.

Some Things Never Change

❖

Have you heard about the man whose creative wife was constantly rearranging the furniture in their house? He never knew where his favorite chair (with pipe and slippers) would be when he came home from work, or in which corner he would find the TV and stereo. He didn't complain much until one night following his shower, without turning on the light, he took a playful leap onto his bed, sailed straight through the screened window, and landed flat on his stomach on the porch roof. The bed had been moved - *re*moved. Fortunately, he suffered no ill effects except for his pride, which was sorely wounded. After that, (in lieu of a divorce) he insisted that whenever (*if ever*) anything was moved, his wife would leave a schematic drawing in plain view on the kitchen counter top, delineating any and all changes as they occurred. Although it seems incredulous for anyone to perpetrate or put up with such bizarre behavior, we must admit that life is full of surprises; some good and some not so good. During these vacillating times, there are at least three Scriptural principles which will bless our hearts. They are true and irrevocable.

1. God is in Control - King Nebuchadnezzar forgot that. He tried to usurp power over the Most High God and was brought low before the prophet Daniel who refreshed his memory saying, "All the inhabitants of the earth are reputed as nothing; He does according to *His* will in the army of heaven and among the inhabitants of the earth. No one can restrain His hand or say to Him, 'What have you done?' " (Daniel 4:35). Another portion of God's Word, the entire 38th Chapter of Job, is taken up with the revealed omnipotence of God. He quizzes Job in Chapter 38:4 and 7: "Where were you when I laid the foundations of the earth? When the morning stars sang together (*heavenly harmony*), and all the sons of God shouted for joy?" Search the scriptures. No matter what, a sovereign God controls it all.

2. God is Good - The Psalmist counsels us, "give thanks to the Lord, for He is good! For His mercy endures forever" (Psalm l07:l). "Good and upright is the Lord" (Psalm 25:8). Nahum l:7 assures us, "The Lord is good, a stronghold in the day of trouble; and He knows those who trust in Him." When others plot to harm us, remember Genesis 50:20, "you meant evil against me; but God meant it for good. Now therefore, do not be afraid." As Joseph spoke to his brothers after they had betrayed him, so God speaks to us. We are urged to, "taste and see that the Lord is good" (Psalm 34:8). We *know* that His plans for us are good according to Jeremiah 29:II, "For I know the thoughts that I think toward you, says the Lord, thoughts of peace and not of evil, plans to give you a future and a hope."

3. God Loves You - How much? The Apostle John writes in John 3:I6, "For God so loved the world that He gave His only begotten Son, that whoever believes in Him should not perish, but have everlasting life." 1 John 3:I says, "Behold what manner of love the Father has bestowed on us, that we should be called children of God!" I John 4:I0 says, "In this is love, not that we loved God, but that He loved us and sent His Son to be the propitiation for our sins." I John 4:I9 says, "We love Him because He first loved us." The Apostle Paul writes in Romans 5:8, "But God demonstrates His own love toward us, in that while we were still sinners, Christ died for us." If that isn't love........You may not identify with the man whose wife was *addicted* to changing furniture, but there will be times when uncertainty is rife on your horizon.

When you just can't figure things out, stop and ask: "Who is really in control here? Is He good? Does He want the best for my life? How much does He love me? Is it enough to get me over this hurdle?" Make your own list of affirmative Bible verses. You will conclude: I. God is in control. 2. God is good. 3. God loves you. These things never change.

"For I am the LORD, I do not change; therefore you are not consumed, O sons of Jacob." (Malachi 3:1)

Song of the Brook

❖

"For He shall give His angels charge over you…In their hands they shall bear you up, lest you dash your foot against a stone." (Psalm 91:11-12)

Approximately fifty feet east of our home, the Oswego River flows quietly by. It is one of the few rivers in the world which flows north rather than south. We might walk out to the edge of the cliff and tumble into it, if we could not see it. Undercurrents determine its velocity, whether it will be calm or swift, but the river is noiseless. "Ole' Man River, Dat ole' man river, he must know somethin' but don't say nuthin', he just keeps rollin' along," laments the old Southern Spiritual. About the same distance to the north, flows a spring-fed brook which ultimately becomes part of the river. It gurgles and splashes happily over the stones, making such melodious sounds that we are compelled to stop and listen, mesmerized by its rhythm.

Its comforting cadence has lulled my restless soul into deep, peaceful slumber on many a summer's night.

What's the difference between the river and the brook? Stones. Without the stones, the brook would lose it song. As part of an agricultural experiment in England, all stones were removed from a plot of farmland. Crops were then planted. The result? Disaster! The harvest was practically nil. This exercise in futility quickly dispelled any and all doubts as to the necessity of rocks in the soil. They provide drainage, warmth, and a healthy balance for young plants, fostering growth. God is not surprised at these scientific findings. Plants and people need balance. He understands that no matter how "spiritual" our intent, it's the rocks and pebbles along the way that turn our hearts toward Him, enabling us to grow and mature. Job put it succinctly: "Man is born to trouble as the sparks fly upward." That being the rule of thumb, shall we grumble, allowing those *troublesome* stones to become stumbling blocks, or should we praise God and thank Him for endowing us with *stepping* stones that can lead to a productive, victorious life?

The Apostle Paul chose to "glory in tribulations, knowing that tribulation produces perseverance; and perseverance, character; and character, hope..." (Romans 5:3-4 KJV). Trials *produce* something; they "work" out perseverance, character and hope (patience, experience and hope). And this hope does not disappoint us; it *satisfies* because the love of God has been poured out in our hearts by the Holy Spirit. As we partake of Christ's sufferings, we learn more of His grace.

Anne Johnson Flint capsules this truth beautifully when she penned: "He giveth more grace when the burdens grow greater, He sendeth more strength when the labors increase." When the love of God is poured out over our heartaches—the pebbles and stones in life—we will radiate joy and tranquility. We will not only be blessed, but we will be a blessing to those about us. "He set my feet upon a rock, and established my steps, He has put a new song in my mouth" (Psalm 40:2-3).

Dear Father, let the stones in our paths give rise to harmony soft and sweet, like the song of the brook.

Sound of Abundance

"Then Elijah said to Ahab, 'Go up, eat and drink; for there is the sound of abundance of rain.' " (1 Kings 18:41)

The sound of abundance. Do we recognize it? Elijah did. For him it spoke of a heavy rain which spelled the end of a three-year drought proclaimed by this fiery prophet of God following his slaughter of 850 heathen prophets. Check out the exciting account of this in 1 Kings 18:16-40. We have no indication that anyone but Elijah heard "the sound of the abundance of rain." We really don't know. It may have been a voice from above or a roar of thunder such as precedes a storm. However, based upon faith (there was not a cloud in the sky), he instructs King Ahab to "go up, eat and drink" while there is still time to avoid the rain. Then Elijah goes up to the top of Mount Carmel to pray and orders his servant to search for a cloud that would come out of the Mediterranean Sea. Back and forth the servant trudged to no avail, until the seventh time when he tells Elijah, "There is a cloud as small as a man's hand rising out of the sea!" (1 Kings 18:44). Soon the sky is black with clouds and wind, followed by a heavy rain and they all saw God answer Elijah's prayer. As the mighty storm approached, the Lord endowed Elijah with power that enabled him to run *before* Ahab's chariot, nearly twenty miles down the mountain to the entrance of Jezreel. What a victory! It is said that even to this day sailors refer to this site as "Cape Carmel."

Consider one precious saint who has battled cancer several times and is again in its tenacious grip as she deals with major surgery for yet another ailment. With a smile on her face and a tear in her eye, she asserts, "I just know that it is going to be alright; things will get better." How does she know? Although Mary does not know what tomorrow holds, she knows Who holds tomorrow. Her confidence springs from the warrant that God is in control at this crucial time. She knows that, "God is our refuge and strength, a very present help in trouble"(Psalm 46:1). She was not always this way, but she has heard the sound of abundance.

Mary's "sound of abundance" led to a final test of faith that was an inspiration to everyone who knew her. She was an all-or-nothing young woman, a natural to win the State championship for her basketball team. She figured that the "ball was in her court" for most of her life. Life had visited many hardships on Mary, beginning when she was a child picking cotton in Louisiana and was punished when her "quota" was unsatisfactory. Later, she met and married an officer in the U.S. Air Force during WW 2, having met him at a USO dance where he played the trumpet in a band. They raised five beloved children. She had become a nurse and learned to depend on her own physical and emotional reserve for climbing the mountains of life. Then she was diagnosed with cancer and given two years to live.

Following her diagnosis, she chose to work in a hospital's med-surgery oncology unit where, because of her affliction, she could "empathize" with others. During this time, a dramatic change took place in Mary's approach to life. Her relationship with Christ took on new and deeper meaning as she learned to depend upon His strength rather than her own. As the storm clouds gathered, she heard the "sound of abundance."

Whereas she was a believer who had always attended church and lived a full life, she claimed that in the midst of her trial, she was experiencing the "more abundant life" which the Lord Jesus had promised. Mary is now at home with her Savior but her life has left an impact on all who had the privilege of knowing her. Another young woman with rheumatoid arthritis is recovering from her thirty-fifth major surgery. Well acquainted with the pain that accompanies such a procedure, she bravely entered the arena bolstered by prayer. There have been tears of pain and tears of joy. Doctors and nurses alike are astounded at the grace and mercy God has poured out on His child as Tudy's recovery takes on miraculous proportions. Never having had an infection from surgery, she knows the sound of abundance well.

What are you up against today? Financial challenges, false accusations, poor health, marital difficulties, misunderstandings, depression, unjust criticism? Elijah's need was rain. Believe God and listen for the sound of abundance in your circumstance. It will enrich your life and it is only a prayer away.

Jesus said, "I have come that they may have life, and that they may have it more *abundantly*." (John 10:10)

Spill My Cup, Lord

✤

"Now hope does not disappoint, because the love of God has been poured out in our hearts by the Holy Spirit who was given to us." (Romans 5:5)

As part of a unique support group which ministers to families in crisis, we were reflecting on some of the outstanding events of the past year during a holiday gathering. What seemed like insurmountable marital problems involving alcohol, drugs and infidelity were brought to the surface in the hope that those present who had experienced like trials could "flesh out" the Scripture as it appears in Colossians 3:15-16. "Let the peace of God rule in your hearts, to which also you were called in one body; and be thankful. Let the word of Christ dwell in you richly in all wisdom, teaching and admonishing one another..." This is called the nouthetic approach to counseling which is derived from the Greek words "nouthesis" or "noutheo" meaning to teach, train or correct Biblically.

So it was, that amidst tears and laughter, armed with God's Word and some of the lessons we had learned, we set out to encourage our brothers and sisters in Christ.

One woman who had struggled long to maintain stability and was on the victory side of a marital crisis, tearfully recounted how the Lord had given her a new heart overflowing with love and joy, so much that when her cup had been jostled earlier in the week, what do you suppose spilled out? Right. It was that same fruit of love and joy, not the bitterness and anger which had controlled her a few months before. She had embraced Biblical principles which enabled her, over a period of time, to create an atmosphere in which her marriage was well on the way toward being healed.

The eighty-year-old father of one of our group further inspired us to set our standards high. We esteemed him a sterling role model. He had been hospitalized, critically ill, yet was bereft of complaints. Nurses, cherishing his words of encouragement, cared for him eagerly, waiting expectantly to hear his favorite phrase, "The Lord is so good to me." His sweet spirit, despite the pain, won the hearts of the medical personnel. A former missionary with New Tribes Missions, his life had not been an easy one, but as his cup spilled over it was found to be a cupful of blessing.

For years I sang and prayed like the woman at the well, "Fill my cup, Lord." I had witnessed many answers to prayer as He gave me "beauty for ashes, the oil of joy for mourning, and the garment of praise for the spirit of heaviness" (Isaiah 61:3). Gradually, my prayer has changed and become, "<u>Spill</u> my cup, Lord." When our plans are thwarted; or grief threatens to overwhelm us; when our cup of life is jarred, may it be God's contagious, unconditional love that *spills* over.

"You prepare a table before me...you anoint my head with oil. My cup runs over." (Psalm 23:5)

Stand

"Position yourselves, *stand* still and see the salvation of the Lord, who is with you." (2 Chronicles 20:17)

There are times in our journey when we get stuck, when we can't do another thing to make life "happen" the way we think it should. The battle is going against us. When all else fails, that's the time to prayerfully turn to God's Instruction Book. We may find that all we need to do is *stand* and wait for further developments.

In a small office fielded by a staff of intelligent but immature women, strife had become the order of the day, every day. Subtle mind games result in lopsided work loads for those who were unwilling to compromise. Consider also a hospital where dedicated nurses are being targeted for ridicule and increased responsibilities by a few conniving dissidents, whose carelessness leads to slipshod, ineffective patient care.

A nuclear engineer sporadically finds valuable papers missing from his desk and replaced by a disturbing note regarding his belief system. Whether at work, at play or somewhere in the daily grind, we are bound to encounter people who can not accept us as we are and who spitefully abuse us for no apparent reason. Personalities clash—call it chemistry—and when they do, battle lines are drawn. Bear in mind that "we do not wrestle against flesh and blood, but against principalities, against powers, against the rulers of the darkness of this age, against spiritual hosts of wickedness" (Ephesians 6:12). Often our struggle becomes a proving ground for character. Filing harassment charges in the workplace may be legitimate in an effort to promote justice, but there is often a creative alternative provided by none other than the God of all Creation.

When the Israelites were sorely afraid of the Egyptians at the Red Sea crossing, Moses told them: "Do not be afraid. *Stand* still, and see the salvation of the Lord, which He will accomplish for you today. For the Egyptians whom you see today, you shall see again no more forever. The Lord will fight for you, and you shall hold your peace" (Exodus 14:13-14). King Saul's son, Jonathan, defeated a great army of Philistines when he considered that the Lord might work on his behalf. "For nothing restrains the Lord from saving by many or by few" (I Samuel 14:6). Numbers in battle are not an issue with God. As Martin Luther said: "One with God is a majority."

King Asa, who reigned in Judah and "did what was good and right in the eyes of the Lord his God," cried out to God and said, "Lord, it is nothing for You to help, whether with many or with those who have no power; help us, O Lord our God, for we rest on You, and in Your name we go against this multitude" (2 Chronicles l4:11). The Lord struck the enemy and they fled. The Lord spoke to King Jehoshaphat of Judah, saying, "Do not be afraid nor dismayed because of this great multitude, for the battle is not yours, but God's...You will not need to fight in this battle. Position yourselves, *stand* still and see the salvation of the Lord, who is with you" (2 Chronicles 15:17). He then appointed singers to sing and praise the Lord God. When they began to sing and to praise, the Lord set ambushes against the enemy and they were defeated. In fact, they helped to destroy one another! (see 2 Chronicles 20:21-23).

Confederate General Thomas Jackson became known as "Stonewall" Jackson during America's Civil War due to his victory at the Battle of Bull Run, Virginia. When it looked as if the Union army had won, Commanding Officer General Cox gave the order to retreat—until he looked across the creek, spotting General Jackson. General Cox stopped short and reversed the order—calling out: "Men, look over yonder. There *stands* General Jackson like a "stone wall." The South won a battle because of a man's *stand.* Incidentally, the general was a Christian.

Raising our voices in praise warrants certain victory, (win or lose) since God inhabits our praise. Satan hates it. Protocol may prevent us from singing and praising audibly in public, but we can position ourselves and *stand*. If we don't *stand* for our faith, we will fall for anything. We are told to be strong in the Lord and in the power of His might, putting on the armor of God that we may be able to *stand* against the wiles of the devil. We need the armor in order to *withstand* in the evil day, and having done all we are to *stand*. Once again in this passage of Ephesians 6:l0-l8, we are admonished to *stand,* wearing the belt of truth. There is no armor for the rear; God is our rearguard (Isaiah 58:8). We are not to run away from our enemies.

As you might have guessed, the office hecklers have become bored with the quiet, firm stance of their chosen quarry and have resorted to squabbling among themselves. They pick at one another's flaws. Those nurses loyal to their profession, as well as the beleaguered secretary have received honorable mention and the devious co-worker has been exposed. Watching your enemies destroy themselves is not a pretty sight. It is doubtful that Queen Esther's cousin, Mordecai, was happy to see wicked Haman hung on the very scaffold he had designed for the execution of Mordecai either (see Esther 7:l0). We are cautioned against rejoicing when our enemy falls. "And do not let your heart be glad when he stumbles;" (Proverbs 24:l7). But divine retribution is as irrevocable as the law of gravity. All we have to do is *stand still and firm* as we wait for God to vindicate us. God saves His own.

"Watch...and pray always that you may be counted worthy...to *stand* `before the Son of Man." (Luke 21:36)

"Whatever you ask in My name, that will I do, so that the Father may be glorified in the Son." (John 14:13)

Stormy Weather

"Immediately He made His disciples get into the boat and go before Him to the other side, while He sent the multitudes away. And when He had sent the multitudes away, He went up on the mountain by Himself to pray...But the boat was now in the middle of the sea, tossed by the waves..." (Matthew I4:22-24)

There are times when we find ourselves in the midst of a painful situation, wondering how we got there and if we will ever get out. Thinking we had carefully charted our course, it appears in retrospect, that we may have misread the map. Take heart. Jesus, aware of the impending storm, sent His disciples directly into it while He went apart to pray. How frightened they must have been. Was our Lord oblivious to their plight? No. "And they cried out for fear. But immediately Jesus spoke to them, saying, 'Be of good cheer! It is I;

do not be afraid" (Matthew 14:26-27) and later delivered them (see Matthew 14:32).

God sends storms of correction and storms of perfection into our lives. When we err, He lovingly disciplines us. When it is time for a growth spurt, He permits a testing period to strengthen us, not to harm us. He cares.

Andrew Murray, a well known theologian, wrote: IN TIMES OF TROUBLE GOD'S TRUSTING CHILD MAY SAY: FIRST. He brought me here. It is by His will I am in this difficult place; in that I will rest. NEXT. He will keep me here in His love and give me grace in this trial to behave as His child. THEN. He will make the testing a blessing, teaching me the lessons He intends for me to learn, and working in me the grace He intends to give. LAST. In His good time He can bring me out again—how and when He knows.

SAY: I am here:

1. By God's appointment
2. In His care
3. Under His training
4. For His time

Having earnestly sought His will through prayer and the Word, we can rest—assured that the Lord has placed us here.

"Call upon Me in the day of trouble; I will deliver you, and you shall glorify Me." (Psalm 50:15)

The Believer's Five Crowns

❖

"And whatever you do, do it heartily, as to the Lord and not to men, knowing that from the Lord you will receive the reward of the inheritance; for you serve the Lord Christ." (Colossians 3:23-24)

B rainstorming is that technique sometimes employed by a group of people for solving problems, or it can be used by individuals for the express purpose of stimulating their thinking. What began as a lark among a group of young people to determine their purpose in life: pursuing worthy goals; developing healthy habits; striving for better "things," soon became a forum for the age-old question, "Why?" The quest put forth by our group was: "What is the purpose behind the activities and events which occupy most of our time and energy these days? Do we act out of pure motives, mixed motives or mainly spur-of-the-moment decisions? Do we aspire to really make a difference in the world or are we operating from a purely retirement mentality? In other words, will the benefits of what we are doing with our lives allow us enough money on which to retire comfortably? How does what we do figure into God's plans for His own?"

A little research in the "upper realm" turned up some challenging alternatives for us to consider. The fact that the Bible offers five rewards or crowns for those God calls His own gave us cause to sharpen our focus and to consider living with more of eternity's values in view.

"For no other foundation can anyone lay than that which is laid, which is Jesus Christ. Now if anyone builds on this foundation with gold, silver, precious stones, wood hay, straw, each one's work will become clear; for the Day will declare it, because it will be revealed by fire; and the fire will test each one's work, of what sort it is. If anyone's work which he has built on it endures, he will receive a *reward*. If anyone's work is burned, he will suffer loss; but he himself will be saved, yet so as through fire" (1 Corinthians 3:11-15).

The Incorruptible Crown is referenced in 1 Corinthians 9:25. "And everyone who competes for the prize is temperate in all things. Now they do it to obtain a perishable (incorruptible-KJV) crown, but we for an imperishable (incorruptible-KJV) crown." The Apostle Paul likens his stance to that of an athlete in the Grecian games where a rigorous program of diet and exercise was the norm. Runner and boxer were both dead set on winning. We are challenged to refrain from worldly lusts, and to conduct our lives in a way that will measure up to our presentation of the Gospel. This means giving ourselves over to such disciplines as worship, study, prayer, sobriety, and loving our neighbor. As Paul said, "All things are lawful for me, but all things are not helpful" (I Corinthians 6:l2). Our liberty in Christ should never be an occasion to cause a brother or sister to stumble. We must walk the talk to receive this prize.

The Crown of Rejoicing or Soul Winner's Crown is referenced in 1 Thessalonians 2:l9-20. "For what is our hope, or joy, or crown of rejoicing? Is it not even you in the presence of our Lord Jesus Christ at His coming? For you are our glory and joy." Some of us may never lead a soul directly to Christ for salvation. Perhaps we have prayed faithfully, another has planted a seed and someone else watered it. Then there comes that moment of decision when the Holy Spirit may cause still another person to come alongside and reap a harvest where he has not sown. Whether we planted the seed, watered it with years of tears, or led that person in the sinner's prayer, we will all share in the party that the angels are hosting in Heaven. "There is joy in the presence of the angels of God over one sinner who repents" (Luke l5:l0). Although God alone gives the increase and He will not share His glory with anyone, many of His children will "come again rejoicing, bringing in the sheaves" (Psalm 126:6) to receive their "Crown of Rejoicing" or the Soul Winner's Crown.

The Crown of Life or the Martyr's Crown is referenced in James 1:12. "Blessed is the man who endures temptation (trial); for when he has been approved, he will receive the crown of life which the Lord has promised to those who love Him." This was written by Jesus' brother, James, primarily to Jewish Christians who were being subjected to persecution. History records that James was martyred a short time after writing this. Even in this present age many people are suffering in record numbers for the cause of Christ. "Do not fear any of those things which you are about to suffer. Indeed, the devil is about to throw some of you into prison, that you may be tested...be faithful unto death and I will give you the crown of life" (Revelation 2:10). The Apostle John wrote this to all believers, but more specifically to the Asian Church of Smyrna, of which Bishop Polycarp was an early martyr. This trophy is for those who love the Lord more than their own lives.

The Crown of Glory or the Elder's Crown is referenced in 1 Peter 5:1-4. "The elders who are among you I exhort, I who am a fellow elder and a witness of the sufferings of Christ, and also a partaker of the glory that will be revealed... Shepherd the flock of God which is among you, serving as overseers, not by compulsion but willingly, not for dishonest gain but eagerly; nor as lords over those entrusted to you, but being examples to the flock; and when the Chief Shepherd appears, you will receive the crown of glory that does not fade away." What a fine example of humble servitude Peter displays here. He considers himself merely a fellow elder even though he had seen Christ's glory at the Transfiguration; walked with Jesus and was a pillar of the church at Jerusalem. Those who humbly tend, feed, and shepherd the flock for the *right* reasons are in line for the Crown of Glory.

The Crown of Righteousness is referenced in 2 Timothy 4:8. "Finally, there is laid up for me the crown of righteousness, which the Lord, the righteous Judge, will give to me on that Day, and not to me only, but also to all who have loved His appearing." The Apostle Paul refers to that event known as the rapture when Christ comes back for His own. This crown is set apart for those who are looking forward to His return. Even so, come, Lord Jesus.

What shall we do with these prizes? Do we vaunt them as badges of honor, in a pompous display? Unquestionably, no! Heaven would lose its luster. As we read in Revelations, He alone is worthy to receive our crowns.

"For the Son of Man will come in the glory of His Father with His angels, and then He will reward each according to his works." (Matthew I6:27)

"For we must all appear before the judgment seat of Christ, that each one may receive the things done in the body, according to what he has done, whether good or bad." (2 Corinthians 5:10)

This Ole' House

❖

"Therefore as the Holy Spirit says: 'Today, if you will hear His voice, do not harden your hearts as in the rebellion.'"

(Hebrews:3:7-8)

"This Ole' House," one of the top ten hit songs of yesteryear, was written by Stuart Hamblen. It aptly depicts the decline of our bodies in the autumn and winter of life. In which season are you? Springtime of youth? Golden years of autumn or winter? Often the lives of the very young are snuffed out in tragic automobile accidents, AIDS and drug related incidents. None of us, young or old, knows how much time we have on Planet Earth.

Years ago, at the time of Billy Graham's first Los Angeles Crusade, Stuart Hamblen invited the evangelist to guest star on his two-hour radio talk show. (He hosted one of the earliest talk shows in Hollywood.) Dr. Graham described Hamblen as a "rootin'- tootin', 6'2, 200 pound cowboy singer." Of no small acclaim, he boasted that his endorsement of Dr. Graham's crusade would guarantee a full house. The evangelist deliberated for some time before accepting the offer to take part in this rather worldly endeavor. Although Billy Graham describes Stuart as rough, strong, loud and earthy in his autobiography "Just As I Am," Dr. Graham liked Stuart and "coveted him for Christ."

On the first night of the Crusade the star left in a huff, convicted of his sin. He kept coming back even though he once got so angry that he shook his fist at Billy on his way out of the tent. The Crusade continued and at 4:30 one morning, Dr. Graham received a phone call from "a voice broken by tears" asking if he could come and talk. It was Stuart Hamblen. Ruth Graham, Grady Wilson and his wife immediately covered the meeting with prayer. The cowboy gave his life to Christ in a "childlike act of faith," according to Billy Graham. Right away, the story goes, he called a Methodist preacher in Texas—his father! What a celebration that must have been! Soon after that, Stuart wrote a song that was inspired by a conversation with his friend, John Wayne, who asked him how he had broken his drinking habit. He gave all the credit to the Lord, stating that He could do it for anyone.

He said, "It's no secret what God can do."

That night, as the clock struck midnight, the now familiar strain ran through his mind. He sat down at the piano and in exactly seventeen minutes finished the melody and words to the country gospel song, "It Is No Secret What God Can Do." Later on he wrote, "This Ole' House," a country western allegory picturing the believer as he sheds his "house," his shell and moves on to his eternal dwelling. He no longer needs this ole' house; he leaves in a hurry. It's too late to close the windows and door. We may be called to our eternal dwelling place without warning. This truth is hardly new.

Ecclesiastes Chapter 12 refers to the uncertainty accompanying old age. "In the day when the keepers of the house (hands, feet) tremble...when the grinders (teeth) cease because they are few...those that look through the windows (eyes) grow dim" (Ecclesiastes 12:3). The verse exhorts us to, "Remember your Creator before the silver cord is loosed, or the golden bowl is broken, or the pitcher shattered at the fountain, or the wheel broken at the well (in other words, the whole circulatory system of the blood ceases to function)."

Old or young, the question is the same—have you given your heart to Jesus Christ? Do you trust in Him? Is He Lord of your life?

"Behold, now is the accepted time; behold, now is the day of salvation." (2 Corinthians 6:2)

House Blessing

God, bless this house, accept our thanks;

Although the mortgage be the bank's;

Lest we forget in quest of goals,

Thou hast the mortgage on our souls.

Toiling and Straining
AKA Doing Our Own Thing

❖

"Now when evening came, the boat was in the middle of the sea; and He was alone on the land. Then He saw them (the disciples) straining at rowing, for the wind was against them. Now about the fourth watch of the night He came to them, walking on the sea, and would have passed them by." (Mark 6:47-48)

There they were—the twelve—it was evening. They had just come from a huge open air picnic, where Jesus had miraculously fed well over five thousand souls with nothing but "five loaves of bread and two fishes" (see Mark 6:33-43). We find these hand-picked protégés of Jesus desperately trying to work their way out of a bad situation. They were "toiling in rowing; straining at rowing" (NAS); "straining at the oars" (NIV); the Amplified Bible states, "they were troubled and tormented in rowing, for the wind was against them." Where was Jesus?

282

Not far away. He saw them—be mindful—He's ever watching. He sees and has compassion on His own. Since the disciples did not heed Him, however, He almost passed them by.

Where is Jesus when we hurt or when we are faced with what seems to be an insurmountable problem? He is close by. What are our options? We can try frantically to make things happen—pushing, pulling, toiling, straining, scrambling— to get out of the web of our circumstance. That's what the disciples did. Sounds logical doesn't it when we think we are sinking? But Jesus gives us another option. We can turn to Him first; we can pray and tell it to Jesus. "Let us therefore come boldly to the throne of grace, that we may obtain mercy and find grace to help in time of need" (Hebrews 4:16).

Peter sets an example for us in Matthew 14:29, responding when Jesus said, "Come," he walked on the water. As soon as he took his eyes off Jesus he began to sink and he sent up an arrow prayer, one of the shortest on record: "Lord, save me!" and Jesus did (Matthew I4:29-31).

When the occasion warrants, God may delegate immediate action in ordering our steps. Or we may find that His timetable includes waiting for an appointed time. If we are so busy "doing our own thing" that we forget to pray, we could by-pass Jesus. We can be certain, however, that He will *not* pass by us! Since Jesus is our high priest and understands our temptations and sympathizes with our weaknesses, "Let us therefore come boldly to the throne of grace, that we may obtain mercy and find grace to help in time of need" (Hebrews 4:16). The Amplified reads: "Let us then fearlessly and confidently and boldly draw near to the throne of grace (the throne of God's unmerited favor to us sinners), that we may receive mercy [for our failures] and find grace to help in good time for every need [appropriate help and well-timed help, coming just when we need it]." One wise servant of God advised: "When you need help in twenty minutes, don't start looking for it in ten." Literally, God sends help just "in the nick of time."

We may be tempted to scoff at the disciples' frenzied attempts, in view of the great miracle they had just witnessed, but what about us? We often assume a "Jehovah complex" when we struggle to "fix" our problem before we ask God for help. Ruth, a young mother whose tests (MRI) led to a diagnosis of a "bubble" on a vein at a crucial spot in her brain, asked for prayer. A few days later when doctors sought out a course of action, they found no trace of the "bubble." Isn't it just like God to do that? Why are we surprised when God answers prayers like this? We shouldn't be. We live in an age of miracles. Still, our baser instincts often lead us to react as the disciples did, "straining and toiling" in a tight situation. Let us call on Jesus when trouble strikes, and consider that this is just another opportunity to trust God.

"Trust in the Lord with all your heart, and lean not on your own understanding; in all your ways acknowledge Him, and He shall direct your paths." (Proverbs 3:5-6)

"He who trusts in the Lord, mercy shall surround him."

(Psalm 32:10)

Turn Your Heart Part 1: Jacob

❖

"And he (Isaac) said, 'Here I am. Who are you, my son?'
Jacob said to his father, 'I am Esau, your firstborn'"

(Genesis 27:18-19)

G enesis Chapter 25 gives us an account of Jacob and
Esau, twin sons born to the patriarch Isaac and his
wife, Rebekah. The firstborn twin was a hairy little fellow
named Esau (hairy). Jacob was delivered last; his hand
clutched his brother's heel, so he was named Jacob, which
meant "supplanter" (deceiver, heel grasper). Fishermen claim
that there is no need to cover their bait buckets when they
are using crabs for bait. One crab will grab the foot of another
when its enterprising counter part attempts to climb out, dragging it back down to a common plane, the bottom. Have you
ever been exposed to people who use unscrupulous methods
to bring others down to their level? They are merely exhibiting
"crabby" behavior.

During Bible times, children were often named some time after birth according to a character trait or a pertinent circumstance. This is still a common practice in countries in the Far East. During his earlier years, we might consider Jacob a scoundrel; a rascal. Deceiving became a way of life for him. Conniving to obtain his elder brother Esau's birthright and blessing, he enticed him in a moment of weakness to exchange his rightful heritage for a pot of porridge (probably lentils) which his mother had concocted with this plan in mind. Esau traded a much coveted double blessing with possible eternal values for an immediate, temporal need. Thus, he "despised his birthright" (Genesis 25:34). Beware, lest we fall into such a snare. Next to become ensnared in Jacob's well-woven web was his father, Isaac. Mother Rebekah contrived with her favorite son (woe to the parents who pit one of their siblings against another), mapping out a plan for him to masquerade as Esau before his blind father. It worked. Jacob went to Isaac at his deathbed and when his father asked, "Who are you, my son?" Jacob said, "I am Esau, your firstborn." His father believed him and pronounced the blessing (Genesis 27).

Jacob left home under duress; Esau was after his life. He fled to his Uncle Laban's home. Laban would later become his father-in-law. En-route, he had his first real encounter with God, who showed him "Jacob's ladder" with angels ascending and descending to Heaven, and promised to make of him a

mighty nation. He was awestricken. Recognizing God's presence, he anointed the stone which had been his pillow and
called that place Bethel, meaning "house of God" (Genesis
28:19). Jacob's heart had begun to turn toward God.

For the next twenty years, Laban broke promises made to
Jacob; withheld Rachel from him; changed his wages upon
impulse, and deceived him many times. God's Word, the law
of sowing and reaping, was being fleshed out in Jacob's life.
"Do not be deceived, God is not mocked; for whatever a man
sows, that he will also reap" (Galatians 6:7).

There came a time when Jacob yearned to go back home.
His greatest fear was that Esau might attack his family but
his fears were groundless. Both Esau and God were ready to
forgive his trespasses. Nevertheless, he sent gifts on ahead
with his servants in an effort to placate his brother and was
left alone at the ford of Jabbok. There, a "Man" wrestled with
him until daybreak and when it became apparent that "He
did not prevail against him, He touched the socket of his hip;
and the socket of Jacob's hip was out of joint as He wrestled
with Him" (Genesis 32:25). Jacob refused to let the Man go
until He blessed him. "So He (the Man) said to him, 'What is
your name?' He said, 'Jacob. And He said, 'Your name shall
no longer be called Jacob, but Israel, for you have struggled
with God and with men, and have prevailed" (Genesis 32:27-
28). God orchestrated circumstances in such a way as to give

Jacob an opportunity for redemption. Isn't it just like God to do that? He is always waiting to draw us back to Himself. When Jacob passed the test, God changed his name to "Israel" which means "Prince with God."

God recycles our trash and gives us a new name and a new beginning. Years ago Isaac had asked Jacob, "Who are you, my son?" Jacob lied and claimed to be "Esau." When God's messenger knocks on the door of his heart, repeating that same question, it becomes Jacob's moment of truth. This time, though, he answers, "Jacob" completing still another cycle. His struggle with man (Esau) and God was an honest one. His repentance is genuine. In fact, the name "Jacob" has come to mean "successor" or "struggling with God." If we have unfinished business with God, the way to take care of it is to "turn our hearts" back to Him.

"Repent therefore and be converted, that your sins may be blotted out, so that times of refreshing may come from the presence of the Lord." (Acts 3:l9)

Turn Your Heart Part 2: Peter

❖

"Peter followed at a distance. Now when they had kindled a fire in the midst of the courtyard and sat down together, Peter sat among them. And a certain servant girl, seeing him as he sat by the fire, looked intently at him and said, 'This man was also with Him.' But he denied Him…"

(Luke 22:54-57)

T he Apostle Peter was in a most wretched predicament following his denial of Jesus Christ; not once but three times. Luke's Gospel tells us that Peter followed at a distance (followed afar off), inferring that he did not wish to be identified with Jesus. Then he cursed and swore in an attempt to add emphasis to his position (just as men do today). Before condemning Peter for having succumbed to the fear of man, perhaps we should monitor our own heartbeat.

Have we ever denied (with or without words) our stance for fear of being ridiculed, refused or rejected by others?

Whatever our reason for distancing ourselves from the Lord, whether it be for monetary gain or a desire to be popular in the world, that's where apostasy begins. Psalm 118:8, said to be the middle verse in the Bible, states: "It is better to trust in the Lord than to put confidence in man." Many of life's choices hinge on this pivotal truth.

At the Passover meal in the Upper Room, Jesus predicted Simon Peter's betrayal praying for him that his faith would not fail. Notice, He did not pray that Peter would not fail because He knew his heart, just as He knows ours. Peter did fail— miserably—and so do we sometimes. Jesus prayed that his *faith* might not fail; that small seed of faith (perhaps as small as a mustard seed) that lives within us. A seed of faith that was given to us by grace and entwined in a promise that will not die once the Holy Spirit has implanted it (see Ephesians 2:8). Peter's faith had wavered, yet we know that later he "...went out and wept bitterly" (Luke 22:62), and that "godly sorrow produces repentance leading to salvation" (2 Corinthians 7:10). Failure is *not* final.

One morning a few *weeks* later, after the disciples had fished all night at the Sea of Tiberius and caught nothing, Jesus instructed them to cast their nets on the right side of Peter's boat. They obeyed and netted almost more fish than they could handle. When Peter saw Jesus on the shore, he plunged into the sea, eager to be the first to greet His Lord (see John 21:1-8). When they arrived on shore, "they saw a fire of coals there, and fish laid on it, and bread" (John 2l:9). What a "coincidence"! Or was it? Every "coincidence" in a believer's life is designed by God. Peter's first personal encounter with Jesus after playing the traitor is over a "fire of coals." Remember, we left him warming himself over a "fire of coals" at the time of his denial. God will bring us back to our point of debarkation, where we left off to begin a fresh walk with Him if we are willing.

Breakfast over; Jesus is now ready to obliterate the pain of Peter's past.Remember Peter's denial of his Lord three times before the crucifixion? Now, as Jesus addresses him, He asks, "Simon, do you love Me?" Twice He uses the Greek word "agape" (sacrificial love). Each time Peter replies, "Yes, Lord you know that I love You," using the word "phileo" (brotherly love). That is the best Peter has to offer. The third time the question is posed, Jesus employs "phileo" also as though asking merely for His disciple's friendship and Peter responds, "Lord, you know all things. You know that I love 'phileo' You" (see John 21:15-17). There is no need for pretense; no more facade; the matter is settled. Sin has been repented of and resolved—Peter's heart has turned back to God—the cycle completed, and now the sinner is fit for service. Jesus tells Peter now go, "Feed and tend My sheep." What grace! What marvelous grace!

D. L. Moody captured the essence of it when he wrote for our edification: "Marvelous grace of our loving Lord, grace that is greater than all our sin."

"And the Lord said, 'Simon...I have prayed for you that your faith should not fail, and when you have returned to Me, strengthen your brethren'" (Luke 22:32).

If you were on trial
for being a Christian
would there be
enough evidence
to convict you?

Turn Your Heart Part 3: Come to Repentance

✤

"The Lord is not slack concerning His promise, as some count slackness, but is longsuffering toward us, not willing that any should perish but that all should come to repentance." (2 Peter 3:9)

A young college boy—a believer—while contemplating a note placed over his mother's kitchen sink bearing this question, was "convicted" by it. That marked a turning point in his life. He determined to follow Christ and soon developed a strong testimony among his peers.

A certain Christian couple living near a large city were given marching orders to transfer immediately to a faraway hamlet situated in an obscure section of the North Woods. The husband's business had taken him there several years before, and a change in the status quo brought about the need to move there permanently. This new job necessitated a hasty departure. It meant pulling up roots—leaving behind friends, neighborhood, school, church, prior commitments, and starting all over again. Those who have "been there" know the sorrow associated with parting and the apprehension that grips the soul. It was a painful, solemn process—but they placed their trust in God and allowed themselves to meld into their new environment.

Now that it was the two of them versus their new world, they grew closer to God and each other. This resulted in the husband's confession that in this same locale where he had formerly conducted business, he had strayed from the Lord. God had sent them back to the scene of his departure from the faith and had kept them there until the man's walk matched his talk. With God's help, he discarded some ungodly habits and became a much loved Sunday School teacher and confidante to a class of defiant high school boys that nobody else wanted to "tackle." His errant past had paved the way for an empathetic approach to their problems. His witness restored, both he and the boys grew spiritually as God's purpose was realized. Sin, repentance, restoration—a cycle completed.

Vessel Unto Honor Part 1

✤

"But in a great house there are not only vessels of gold and silver, but also of wood and clay, some for honor and some for dishonor." (2 Timothy 2:20)

In the beginning God created heaven and earth; day and night; then separated the sea from the mists of the skies. He spoke into existence grass, herbs, fruit trees; next, the sun, the moon and stars; followed by birds, sea creatures, beasts and creeping things. Then God said, "Let Us make man in Our image, according to Our likeness..." (Genesis I:26). "And the Lord God formed man of the dust of the ground, and breathed into his nostrils the breath of life..." (Genesis 2:7), ushering in the dawn of man's life on earth.

Those who are of a scientific trend of mind, agree that the chemistry of man's body is perfectly aligned with that of the clay from which it was formed. Precisely the same elements—water, calcium, sodium, iron, copper, nitrogen, arsenic, phosphorus, sulphur, carbon, zinc, selenium, etc.—are found in human beings and clay alike. Sequentially, it was not a far cry at all for God to breathe life into these elements, thereby birthing Adam, whose name means "of the ground."

A potter will not waste his time on just any old piece of clay—first it must be carefully chosen; weathered; rested; prepared. The Master Potter does not create "junk" either. We were hand-picked. "He chose us in Him before the foundation of the world..." (Ephesians l:4). "You did not choose Me, but I chose you and appointed you that you should ...bear fruit..." (John l5:l6). He chose and commissioned us to be productive. Chosen.

After choosing the clay, the potter's next objective is to "weather" it. Stormy weather is a necessary part of ecological balance. Disturbances in the elements are what weed out the chaff. When troubles seem to pelt us like stones in a hailstorm, it helps us to remember that. And storms are seasonal. They don't last forever. Life without problems would be like a sky without clouds. Too much sunshine makes a desert and deserts do not bear fruit. Life is like a grindstone. Its trials are not meant to wear us down, but to sharpen and polish us up! God spoke to Peter, James and John from a *cloud* on the Mount of Transfiguration, announcing: "This is My beloved Son, in whom I am well pleased. Hear Him!" (Matthew l7:5). So it was from a *cloud* that Christ's identity was first revealed to the disciples at the beginning of His ministry, and it is from the *cloud* that Jesus will come at last to take us up to be with Him in the air (see 1Thessalonians 4:l7). Weathering is a prerequisite for a sound vessel.

Next, the potter rests and tests the clay. We may be detained against our will in what seems like a state of limbo. This process cannot be rushed. We often feel like an obscure book on a shelf when we are in God's waiting room. A certain young man, as a result of a rebellious, non-conformist life, has found himself literally restrained under prison guard. Yet he realizes that he is precisely where God wants him to be. During this time that he is set aside (rested—tested), he is choosing to submit to the loving hands of the Potter, with the hope of a new beginning—becoming a vessel unto honor, one which God can use.

"If anyone cleanses himself…he will be a vessel for honor, sanctified and useful for the Master, prepared for every good work." (2 Timothy 2:2l)

Vessel Unto Honor Part 2:
A Work in Progress

"The word which came to Jeremiah from the Lord, saying: 'Arise and go down to the potter's house, and there I will cause you to hear My words.' Then I went…and there he was, making something at the wheel. And the vessel that he made of clay was marred in the hand of the potter; so he made it again into another vessel, as it seemed good to the potter to make." (Jeremiah 18:1-4)

V erse 4 of Jeremiah 18 is a portrait of creation and redemption: man was made by God; marred by sin; then re-made according to His original design (see 2 Corinthians 5:17, Colossians 3:10). Once the potter has chosen the clay for his project (each of us is a "project under construction"), and weathered it with just the right amount of water, heat and cold; rested and tested it tentatively, he must identify his creation before he can move on. Shall he create a vase to embellish a bouquet of daffodils or a basin like the one in which Jesus washed the disciples' feet? Shall he use his skill to mold a beautiful teapot or will he call it a dazzling work of art? He makes a decision; then he names the vessel.

Jesus called each one of us by our name before we were created. "But now, thus says the Lord, who created you, O Jacob, and He who formed you, O Israel: 'Fear not, for I have redeemed you; I have called you by your name; You are mine" (Isaiah 43:l). "I have even called you by your name; I have named you, though you have not known Me" (Isaiah 45:4). We were "made in secret, and skillfully wrought in the lowest parts of the earth." The Master Potter saw our substance before it was formed (see Psalm l39:15-16), and named us accordingly. He knew the shape of our eyes and nose. He knew the purpose for which He would create us. "Everyone who is called by My name, whom I have created for My glory; I have formed him, yes, I have made him" (Isaiah 43:7). God fashioned us after His image, so each one of us has intrinsic worth. The potter's hands will knead and knead, push and pull, stretch the clay and with tenderness but firmness, and will slam it back down toward the moving wheel whenever a destructive air pocket or bubble appears. Our defect (bubble) may take on the form of anger, bitterness, envy or greed. The clay cannot correct its own flaw; the potter must do it. So it is with God and us. How many times have we been s-t-r-e-c-h-e-d? Or maybe we were uplifted to a mountain top experience only to fall flat on our faces. "Why is this happening?" we groan. Sometimes the Potter needs to take drastic action to shape us and break us. It might be chastisement or it may simply be part of the weathering process we need to develop our character. Key to this phase is the potter's liberal use of water to produce just the right texture necessary for smoothing off a rough edge or squeezing out an air pocket. According to Ephesians 5:26, God cleanses and sanctifies us with the "washing of water by the Word" that He might present us to Himself a glorious church not having spot or wrinkle or any such thing. Ample application of water warrants a sturdy blemish-free vessel. If we can visualize ourselves as a work in progress in the Master's Hands, we will more readily accept our stretches and let-downs, not as regressions but as part of His design to strengthen and stabilize us.

"But may the God of all grace, who called us...after you have suffered awhile, perfect, establish, strengthen, and settle you." (I Peter 5:l0)

Vessel Unto Honor Part 3: Tested by Fire

"In this you greatly rejoice, though now for a little while, if need be, you have been grieved by various trials, that the genuineness of your faith, being much more precious than gold that perishes, though it is tested by fire, may be found to praise, honor, and glory at the revelation of Jesus Christ." (I Peter I:6-7)

Assume that the potter has chosen the clay for his "masterpiece;" exposed it to variations of weather necessary for its survival; rested and tested it; identified and named it; shaped and re-shaped it when it was marred; perhaps molded it again and again "at the wheel" (Jeremiah I8:I-4), until he is satisfied with the appearance of his precious creation. He is aware that there is one more element to which the clay must submit before its purpose can be accomplished. It must be tested by fire, not once but twice. The vessel must be "fired" within the confines of a kiln's intense heat in order for its potential beauty—its color and texture—to be brought to the surface. Extreme heat is also an essential factor in producing a completely water-resistant vessel. This "firing" is the final test for determining the usefulness, beauty and value of the potter's endeavor.

The Apostle Paul prayed that the Philippian church would be "sincere" and without offense (or blemish) until the day of Christ (Philippians I:l0). In that day, the Latin word "sincera" (meaning without wax) was etched on any vessel that had been tested by fire and proved to be genuine. This insignia would deter a potter from deceiving his client by filling a hairline crack with wax, and selling him a cracked pot. Of course, the wax would melt with exposure to heat. It is from this same word "sincera" that we get our word "sincere." Are we worthy of the label "sincere" or will we crack under pressure when fiery trials assail us? Malachi 3:2-3 declares, "For he is like a refiner's fire...He will sit as a refiner and a purifier of silver; He will purify the sons of Levi, and purge them as gold and silver, that they may offer to the Lord an offering in righteousness." While the fire is transforming the vessel, the potter rarely takes his eyes off it. "Firing" (heating) the ore to a certain temperature causes impurities to rise to the surface, purging it. The potter sits over a fiercely heated vat of silver or gold, using an instrument that rakes off the dross as it comes to the surface.

The refiner (potter) repeats this process again and again, all the while looking down into the heated metal. When he sees a perfect reflection of his face, minus those specks and flaws which were in the ore at the beginning, he knows that the purification process is complete. The gold and silver are then removed from the heat.

The eyes of our Potter tenderly watch over us in much the same way. We are being transformed as He awaits a clearer reflection of His likeness. He is in the fire with us just as surely as He was with Daniel's three friends, Shadrach, Meshach and Abed-Nego centuries ago. " 'Did we not cast three men bound into the midst of the fire?' asked King Nebuchadnezzar. They answered, 'True, O king.' 'Look', he answered, 'I see four men loose, walking in the midst of the fire; and they are not hurt, and the form of the fourth is like the Son of God' " (Daniel 3:24-25). He goes with us into the furnace of affliction. When our trial is complete, when the crucible has done its work—conforming us to the image of His Son—He will deliver us.

Everything that happens to us is "Father-filtered." We cannot experience God to the fullest until we have allowed His hands to mold us and leave His fingerprints of love on our lives. Let us then submit to the Potter's sensitive hands, that we may be a "vessel for honor, sanctified and useful for the Master, prepared for every good work" (2 Timothy 2:2I).

Wages of Death or Gift of Life?

❖

"For the wages of sin is death; but the gift of God is eternal life through Jesus Christ our Lord." (Romans 6:23)

T he motto on a police station wall sometime ago proclaimed: *"Crime doesn't pay."* The truth is that crime *does* pay guaranteed wages—death. Sin holds the same promise—death by doing. While we may not reap a harvest immediately, "it is appointed for men to die once, but *after this* the judgment" (Hebrews 9:27). That would be bad news except for the Good News, "that God has given us eternal life, and this life is in His Son" (1 John 5:11). We can go to hell without doing anything really bad, because we are sinners by nature. We have inherited Adam's sin nature. Paradoxically however, doing good will not get us to Heaven either. It is only as we "believe" (trust in; adhere to; rely on) Jesus Christ, God's only Son who died for our individual sins, that we may expect to live eternally with Him. The dismal fact is that there are many people who literally *choose* the path that leads to damnation and hell by rejecting God's gift of salvation. History is replete with testimonies bearing the mark of their choices: some wise, some not so wise.

Dwight L. Moody, (Moody Bible Institute) the 19th Century evangelist who began by organizing Sunday school classes in the poor neighborhoods in Chicago, preached Christ to more than an estimated 100 million people before radio and television made mass audiences common. He died in 1899, his last words being: "This is glorious! Earth recedes; Heaven is opening; God is calling me."

Voltaire, the famous French author-philosopher-historian of the 1700's "Enlightenment" period, predicted that the Bible would become extinct in fifty years. He wrote essentially that many Jews from the "rabble" had played at being prophets and that Jesus was one that made more noise than the others, and who was turned into a god. As Voltaire lay dying he cried out, "I am abandoned by God and man; I shall go to hell!" After his demise, Voltaire's estate in France became a publishing house for the Book of Books, the Bible.

Dr. M.R. DeHaan, physician and founder of the Radio Bible Class (Our Daily Bread), knew he was on the brink of death in 1965. He had nearly died with a heart attack but had been revived and was somewhat disappointed, reflecting that he longed to be with Jesus. He shared with his friend Henry

Bosch as they viewed the Thornapple River flowing placidly behind DeHaan's home: "Yes, it is magnificent, but everything looks different and even more beautiful when you're standing right on the brink!"

Bertrand Russell, Nobel Peace Prize winner in 1950, propagated his atheist views far and wide. Just before his death in 1970, he was quoted as saying: "There is darkness without and when I die there will be darkness within. There is no splendor, no vastness anywhere, only triviality for a moment – then nothing!"

John Wanamaker, Christian philanthropist and founder of the first large-scale department store in America and credited with making the first penny-bank, said: "Dying is just like opening the door, and going into my Father's house." **Napoleon Bonaparte,** the "Little General," reminisced near the end of his life (1821): "Alexander, Caesar, Charlemagne and myself founded empires. But on what did we rest the creations of our genius? Upon force. Jesus Christ alone founded His empire upon love; and at this hour, millions of men would die for Him."

Charles H. Spurgeon, the man many in the19th century referred to as the "Prince of Preachers," is probably the most oft quoted of all men by pastors in our pulpits today. He built the Metropolitan Tabernacle, the largest church on earth in its time, where each week some five thousand people crowded in to hear him. Innumerable souls were converted under his ministry through sermons, books, periodicals and publications which were distributed all over the world. During the illness that would end his life he said: "My theology now is found in four little words: 'Jesus died for me.' I don't say this is all I would preach if I were to be raised up again, but it is more than enough for me to die upon." In 1Timothy 3:16 it tells us that, "God was manifested in the flesh, and received up in glory." Spurgeon said that if we would joy in Christ's glory hereafter, He must be glorious in our sight now. Can you say that He is in your life today? It's our choice.

Blaise Pascal, a noted philosopher, mathematician, and theologian, was asked as he lay near death, "What has impressed you most in your life about the Bible and your walk with God?" Pascal is quoted as saying, "Jesus loves me; this I know. For the Bible tells me so."

"For God so loved the world that He gave His only begotten Son, that whoever believes in Him should not perish but have everlasting life." (John 3:16)

Walk and Not Faint

"But those who wait on the Lord shall renew their strength; they shall mount up with wings like eagles; they shall run and not be weary, and they shall walk and not faint."

(Isaiah 40:31)

"I would just like to run and get it over with quickly," my friend blurted out, as we pondered a trial that she was going through. She had *not* run, however, but had chosen to "wait" on the Lord, as opposed to taking the world's way out. The word "wait" in this portion of Isaiah comes from a Hebrew word *qavah* which means "to bind together by twisting." We may think of it as a rope - the threads so tightly woven together that it is practically unbreakable. When our lives become intertwined and woven together with God's plan for us, we will actually gain strength during our "waiting" period. We "shall run and not be weary; and we shall walk and not faint."

As new Christians, do we not mount up with wings as eagles, fledglings following an erratic pattern, eager to share our new found faith with everyone? This phase usually accompanies our first love. Next, while we are still young in the Lord, we may run and not be weary—settling down a bit—as our faith begins to grow. The last phase is our everyday walk. Although there is joy in the journey, it may not be particularly glamorous. Some will be called upon to walk a lonely path for a while. Whereas we may experience occasional "highs" and "lows" we find ourselves—in general—on a steady, more even keel. God is teaching us to "walk and not faint" while we wait on Him. It's a maturing process.

A lovely woman in India, a Hindu convert, has been tortured unmercifully for her stand in Christ. She has since become a missionary to her people. Nissi's ears, as well as her nose had been cut off by her husband before he fled to England with their child. This was the penalty that she paid for professing her Christian faith and getting baptized. Plastic surgery has compensated for much of her disfigurement. As I would have consoled her, Nissi's eyes brimmed with tears and she said: "Sister, my suffering was but for a short time. The real test is the witness of a day-by-day walk with Jesus Christ." Then she smiled her radiant, victorious smile. Nissi which means, "The Lord is My Banner," walks and does not faint. Nissi continues to "wait on the Lord" and walk steadfastly with Him. She is in a good place. Who but God can give us renewed spiritual strength while we wait?

"The LORD is good to them that wait for Him."

(Lamentations 3:25)

Waterpots of Stone

✥

"Now there were set there six waterpots of stone, according to the manner of the purification of the Jews...Jesus said to them, 'Fill the waterpots with water.' And they filled them up to the brim." (John 2:6-7)

At Jesus' first recorded miracle at the wedding feast in Cana, He said to the servants, "Fill the water pots with water." They immediately did what He told them. He had a higher plan for those waterpots, however, than the traditional purification of the Jews by their frequent ceremonial hand washing before meals. (Who knows the miracles we may have missed because we did not obey Him promptly?)

Apparently friends of Jesus' family were being married, since Jesus, His mother and His disciples were all guests. We have no idea how long they had been there before the supply of wine was depleted. It was customary for wedding celebrations to last up to seven days. For example, Samson posed a riddle to his male guests, challenging them to solve it within "the seven days of the feast" and later we find that his wife "had wept... the seven days while their feast lasted." (Judges 14:12-17). It is still common in Far East places like India for festivities surrounding a marriage to continue for days with the house guests remaining with the family for several weeks following a wedding. So there may be times when the host's supply of food and drink is exhausted.

Do you have or do you know someone whose heart is as cold as stone, and as empty as those waterpots were? Blaise Pascal described man's heart as a "God-shaped vacuum, which only He can fill." Our efforts to fill that void have led us to self-helps, self-will, self-confidence, and even self-condemnation. In order to make room for God and the Holy Spirit in our hearts, we must be emptied of *ourselves.* The empty wedding vessels were filled with water, a symbol of the Holy Spirit. In John 7:38-39, Jesus said, " 'He who believes in Me, as the Scripture has said, out of his heart will flow rivers of living water.' But this He spoke concerning the Spirit, whom those believing in Him would receive..." The Old Testament prophet, Ezekiel, in dealing with God's renewal of his beloved Israel, declared, "Then I will sprinkle clean water on you, and you shall be clean...I will give you a new heart and put a new spirit within you; I will take the heart of stone out of your flesh and give you a heart of flesh. I will put My Spirit within you and

cause you to walk in My statutes, and you will keep My judg-
ments and do them" (Ezekiel 36:25-27).

Every time one of us submits a cold stony heart to Jesus,
He performs still another miracle. He gives us a *new* heart
of flesh, emptied of self and "filled to the brim" with His Holy
Spirit. Just as water and wine were a source of gratification at
the wedding, so we may become spiritual food and drink for
others as Spirit-filled servants of our Lord and Savior, Jesus
Christ. Let it be so.

Waters of Affliction Waves of Blessing

"And in the fourth watch of the night Jesus went unto them, walking on the sea. And when the disciples saw him walking on the sea, they were troubled, saying, It is a spirit; and they cried out for fear. But straightway Jesus spake unto them, saying, Be of good cheer; it is I; be not afraid."

(Matthew 14:25-27 KJV)

I s your ship being tossed about in a tempestuous sea? Do you seem to be sinking under the waters of affliction? "Be not afraid," Jesus said. The disciples were in just such a predicament when Jesus appeared to them, "walking on the sea." The very thing that they feared most—the waves— which in their finite minds spelled doom, became the vehicle by which He would come to them—to reassure—and finally, to rescue them.

So it is with us. Whatever the tumult in our lives—a child who has run away or one who is hopelessly ensnared in the drug culture or homosexuality; a shattered marriage; a crippling illness or a financial crisis—we have Jesus' words to encourage us: "Be not afraid." So fear not, beloved. When we think we are about to go under we can cry out to Him in confidence, knowing that He will come alongside and draw us closer to Him. When our faith is weak, we must count on His faithfulness to draw us closer to Him. Jesus will surely come to us on the waves of our dilemma, to comfort, deliver and ultimately, to bless us.

He has promised: **"I will never leave you nor forsake you"** (Hebrews 13:5). The intent in the original language might read: "I will never, no never, no never—leave you or forsake you."

Trials

Tempestuous though today appears,
(We'd forgo trials if we could);
We know, in seeing past the tears,
These things—through Christ— Work for our good.

"And we know that all things work together for good to those who love God, to those who are called according to His purpose." (Romans 8:28)

Weeds Among the Wheat

❖

"Another parable He put forth to them, saying: 'The kingdom of heaven is like a man who sowed good seed in
his field; but while men slept, his enemy came and sowed
tares (weeds – NIV) among the wheat and went his way."

(Matthew 13:24-25)

Jesus' wisdom in citing the earthy parable of the tares was
brought forcibly home to me last spring when I learned a
very simple, yet costly lesson from my garden. Vowing to get
a head start on those pesky weeds, I set about plucking them
up by the handful and tossing them aside. Mission accomplished. Weeks later, it was time for "the flowers to appear
on the earth and the time of the singing of the birds is come"
(Song of Solomon 2:12). Melodies burst forth in heavenly
harmony as the songbirds performed right on schedule but
guess what? There were no flowers. My heart sank. In time, a
few hardy little blossoms waved a belated, feeble "hello," but

compared to last year's lush growth, our garden was a "fizzle." It was then that I noticed that nestling close to the sparse blossoms were plants whose leaves were almost identical to the real thing. They had mimicked their "fellow flowers" so well that, laboring under the spell of deceit, I had pulled up most of our "black-eyed-susans" and "magenta colored phlox." Those fraudulent weeds may not have deceived a more experienced gardener. Or would they?

Matthew 24:24 warns us that during the last days "false christs and false prophets will rise and show great signs and wonders to deceive, if possible, *even the elect"* (emphasis added). Because satan is the master of counterfeit and deceit, Jesus forewarned the servants in His parable not to gather up the tares until the harvest, lest they pull up the wheat with the weeds (see Matthew 13:24-25).

Tares (weeds) are those pseudo-Christians or wolves in sheep's clothing who may regularly occupy a pew in any church body. They go through all the motions of a believer deceitfully hiding their true nature. They may live under the guise of Christianity for years. Charlatans, they were sown by the enemy among the wheat. Bible teacher Charles Swindoll explains that sheep and wolves get along together alright until feeding time. Then the wolves eat the sheep. The Apostle Paul wrote to Timothy, "The Lord knows those who are His..." (2 Timothy 2:19).Psalm 1:4 portrays the ungodly as worthless "chaff which the wind drives away." During World War 2, we are told how the Air Force would drop electronic chaff over the enemy's territory for the express purpose of scrambling their signals. Even though this waste product (chaff) would serve a worthy cause in this case, it was still used to deceive and distract. That's the strategy of the enemy.

The Apostle Paul cautioned the Ephesian church to be on the lookout for savage wolves who would come in among them, not sparing the flock (see Acts 20:29). This was written for our admonition also. At harvest time—the end of the age—it will be no chore to distinguish between the weeds and the wheat. If you have ever gazed upon a field of wheat when it is golden ripe, you will note that it is bowed low, heavy with grain. In contrast the empty-headed, prideful weeds stand tall, blowing saucily in the wind. 1John 4:1 instructs us not to believe every spirit, but to "test the spirits, whether they are of God; because many false prophets have gone out into the world." May our spiritual eyes develop the ability to discern between God's beautiful blossoms and their deceitful counterparts.

"Beware of false prophets, who come to you in sheep's clothing, but inwardly they are ravenous wolves. You will know them by their fruits." (Matthew 7:15-16)

What the Gospel Is About

✤

"For I delivered to you first of all that which I also received: that Christ died for our sins according to the Scriptures, and that He was buried, and that He rose again the third day according to the Scriptures." (1 Corinthians 15:3-4)

Instructing the Corinthian believers as to the resurrection of Jesus Christ, the Apostle Paul seems to have captured the gist of the Gospel in a nutshell. The term "gospel" is taken from an Anglo-Saxon word "godspel" meaning good message or good news. And it *is* good news for those who have embraced its truth on a personal level. "If you confess with your mouth the Lord Jesus and believe in your heart that God has raised Him from the dead, you will be saved. For with the heart one believes unto righteousness and with the mouth confession is made unto salvation" (Romans 10:9-10).

Those who have invited Jesus Christ to be Savior and Lord look forward to eternal life and rightly so. If our faith is genuine however, it will be accompanied by a desire to be *good* witnesses so that others will be won to Christ. A sense of responsibility born of that desire will affirm the depth of our faith to an unbelieving world. They will know we are Christians by our love. "You shall love the Lord your God with all your heart, with all your soul, with all your strength, and with all your mind, and your neighbor as yourself" (Luke 10:27). "On these two commandments hang all the Law and the Prophets" (Matthew 22:40). "There is no other commandment greater than these" (Mark 12:31).

When a certain lawyer, in an effort to justify himself, asked Jesus who his neighbor was, Jesus recounted the parable of the good Samaritan (See Luke 10:25-37). A Jewish man on his way to Jericho had been robbed, beaten, stripped of his clothes, and left on the road to die. The road from Jerusalem down to Jericho was a seventeen mile stretch, a sharp decline of about 3200 feet, where robbery and murder was so common that it was called "The Way of Blood" during the first century. Bands of marauders would hide behind the rocks in that barren terrain.

Jesus chose a scenario that would be entirely familiar with the lawyer who was interrogating him. The Bible tells us that the priest was going "down" the Jericho road. The priest and the Levite, both Jews, had probably come from some sort of service at the temple. Actually, they may not have been *bad* men— just *busy* men. They passed him by. Although the Samaritans and Jews hated each other, it was a Samaritan who saw and had compassion on the wounded man. What would Jesus have done? What would you or I have done?

What is the gospel about? It's about the head—our thoughts. Do we really think and pray about a missionary's need? What, if anything, can we do about it? *It's about the heart—the seat of our emotions.* Do we care? The Samaritan did. He stopped, bandaged the injured man's wounds, and brought him on his own animal to an inn. He really *cared* for him. *The gospel is about our hands:* lifting a brother up; a gentle touch; a friendly hug; applying the oil of kindness. In a final act of brotherly love, the Samaritan paid the innkeeper for all accrued expenses. *The gospel is about our checkbook.* For many of us this is the real test. We need not be wealthy to share, although God blesses and multiplies all gifts. A poor widow gave her two mites, and it is recorded in Scripture that she "put in more than all" of those who had already given (Luke 20:3). Whether it is for missions, food cupboards, clothing exchanges, or the guy next door who just lost his job, there will never be a scarcity of needs.

The *gospel* is about our *walk.* Who is my neighbor? Whom can I befriend? Establishing loving relationships will involve personal sacrifice. It is a calculated risk, bound to include interruptions from the Holy Spirit. We need to leave time for Holy

Spirit interruptions. The Samaritan's timetable was greatly altered when he broke journey to minister to his "neighbor." A change in our schedules will be required, perhaps even a discarded day timer, but the rewards are great. As Jesus said, "It is more blessed to give than to receive" (Acts 20:35). It pleases God when we help someone in need, and as a side effect, it *feels* good. In addition, its dividends are eternal. The most humble act of kindness may be just the touch that our neighbor needs to steer him or her toward the Kingdom. It's been said (no irreverence intended) that there are five gospels: Matthew, Mark, Luke, John and you (or me). We may be the only gospel that people ever read. So let's pay attention to God's call and be about our Father's business; that of relating His never-changing Word to an ever-changing world.

"By this all will know that you are My disciples, if you have love for one another." (John 13:35)

Wisdom

S even attributes of wisdom are found in James 3:17. "But the wisdom that is from above is first pure, then peaceable, gentle, willing to yield, full of mercy and good fruits, without partiality and without hypocrisy."

Saturday morning call-to-work was the signal for our church family to come and bring the "tools" with which we felt the most comfortable and might be helpful for the spring clean-up: brooms, mops, scrubbers, paint brushes, vacuum cleaners, garden rakes, etc. We were a cheerful bunch, if a bit ludicrous as we trickled in—one by one—dragging with us various accoutrements pertinent to the job at hand. We gathered for a word from Scripture and prayer before beginning our work detail. Devotions centered around Exodus Chapters 35 and 36, where instructions were given to the Israelites concerning the workmen who would erect the tabernacle. "And let every able and wise-hearted man among you come and make all that the Lord has commanded" (Exodus 35:10 AMP).

"And they came, both men and women, as many as were willing hearted, and brought bracelets, and earrings, and rings, and tablets, all jewels of gold: and every man that offered, offered an offering of gold unto the LORD" Exodus 35:22 (KJV). "All the women who had ability and were 'wise-hearted' spun with their hands, and brought what they had spun..." (Exodus 35:25 AMP). "And all the women who had ability and whose hearts stirred them up in wisdom spun..." (Exodus 35:26 AMP). "And Moses said to the Israelites, 'See, the Lord called by name Bezalel son of Uri, the son of Hur, of the tribe of Judah; And He has filled him with the Spirit of God, with ability and wisdom, with intelligence and understanding, and with knowledge and all craftsmanship' " (Exodus 35:30-31 AMP). "He has filled them with wisdom of heart and ability to do all manner of craftsmanship, of the engraver, of the skillful workman, of the embroiderer in blue, purple, and scarlet [stuff] and in fine linen, and of the weaver, even of those who do or design any skilled work" (Exodus 35:35 AMP)

Exodus 36:I-2 states: "Bezalel and Aholiab and every wise-hearted man in whom the Lord put wisdom and understanding to know how to do all the work for the service of the sanctuary shall work according to all that the Lord has commanded. And Moses called Belzlel and Aholiab and every able and wise-hearted man in whose mind the Lord had put wisdom and ability, every one whose heart stirred him up to come to do the work" (AMP). In Exodus 36:5-6 we are told that the people brought "much more then enough" to complete the work—enough that Moses issued an order restraining the people from bringing any more.

Who is reputed to have been the wisest man in the world? King Solomon, of course; we equate his name with wisdom. I Kings 3:9 makes Solomon's request to God plain: "So give Your servant an understanding mind and a hearing heart to judge Your people, that I may discern between good and bad. For who is able to judge and rule this Your great people?" (AMP). God responds, "Behold, I have done as you asked. I have given you a wise, discerning mind, so that no one before you was your equal, nor shall any arise after you equal to you" (I Kings 3:12 AMP). Finally, I Kings 4:29 sums it up: "God gave Solomon wisdom and very great insight, and a breadth of understanding as measureless as the sand of the seashore" (NIV). Chapter 4 of I Kings ends with an impressive account of Solomon's accomplishments, and states: "he was wiser than any other man..." (1 Kings 4:31 NIV).

Knowledge is an important factor in leading us toward productive lives. Let us garner all we can. Proverbs I4:I8b tells us: "The prudent are crowned with knowledge" (NIV). Proverbs I5:2 says: "The tongue of the wise uses knowledge rightly..." We are cautioned, however, in I Corinthians 8:I: "Knowledge puffeth up..." (KJV). Knowledge is germane to the head...

wisdom to the heart. It would seem then, that head knowledge must be blended with a wise heart to be used effectively. So let us pray with the Psalmist, "Teach us to number our days, that we may apply our hearts unto wisdom" (Psalm 90:12 KJV).

Then, we can come to God—"those who are wise-hearted, those whose hearts have stirred them up in wisdom, those in whom the Lord has put wisdom and understanding"— to join in the work He has called us to do. We can be certain that there will be enough and "much more than enough" to complete the work of cleaning a church, visiting the shut-ins, praying for the lost, loving our neighbor, and in the end, building the Kingdom.

"Bow down thine ear, and hear the words of the wise, and apply thine heart unto my knowledge" (Proverbs 22:17 KJV).

Worst Enemy—Best Friend

❖

"Before I was afflicted I went astray: but now have I kept thy word. It is good for me that I have been afflicted; that I might learn thy statutes." (Psalm 119:67, 71 KJV)

Have you ever regarded your affliction as an ally—a friend? A young wife and mother suffered several years of undiagnosed depression which led to a complete physical and emotional breakdown. In a last desperate attempt to regain soundness of mind and body, she began to read the Bible. God spoke to her through such Scriptures as: "God has not given us a spirit of fear, but of power and of love and of a sound mind" (2 Timothy 1:7). "Then who did?" she reasoned. Obviously, it was the deceiver—the father of lies—the accuser—the devil. The Holy Spirit was at work even though she did not have a personal relationship with the Lord. She began reading the Psalms in an effort to quiet her spirit. A few months later, she joined a small Bible Study group where she received Jesus Christ as her Savior and Lord. Ultimately, He became her Healer from a serious disease. "God is our refuge and strength, a very present help in trouble" (Psalm 46:1). "Trouble," as used here, indicates extreme distress, as in a tight place. The darkness that had enveloped her soul, rather than destroying her life, became the catalyst that led to life eternal for this woman.

A young woman, who was afflicted with rheumatoid arthritis when she was very young, is never completely free from pain. While she does not enjoy it, the pain has actually become her *friend*, she claims, because it serves as a barometer—measuring her need for medication, exercise, etc. She compares her plight with leprosy, where no pain is felt and subsequently, body parts become atrophied and waste away. The absence of pain is the leper's enemy.

Or perhaps your adversary is an unscrupulous character whose life is unavoidably linked with yours, through separation or divorce. Custody "battles" for children are ugly. A mother may seek to protect her child, while the father behaves in a cunning, vindictive manner to undermine her attempts to shield the youngster from emotional harm.

Or the situation may be reversed. Recently, a "mom" was confronted by her friend, with the suggestion that her "difficult person" might prove to be her best friend. She thought this may be right, although at first the idea seemed repugnant. Skirmishes in the ongoing crisis—craftiness and verbal abuse—have caused this mother to delve into God's Word and to seek Christian counsel continuously. By growing spiritually, she has found a way to shield her child and maintain soundness of mind. "Call upon Me in the day of trouble; I will deliver you, and you shall glorify Me" (Psalm 50:15).

Legend has it that a loathsome spider saved a nobleman from certain death. Robert Bruce (or Robert the Bruce, as he was called) was born in Scotland in 1274 AD. Those were the days when the feudal system prevailed in the British Empire. Scottish clans fought against England and sometimes against one another in an effort to regain property rights to their lands which had been confiscated. During one vicious battle, it is reported the enemy had wiped out most of Robert's family, but he escaped. The young man was fleeing on foot from the enemy when he came upon a small cave in one of the highlands of Scotland. He dove into the cave for refuge and waited breathlessly. Crouched down, looking upward, he spied a nearby spider spinning its web. (Have you ever watched a spider weave its wondrous web in just a few minutes?) Not particularly fond of spiders, he was irritated that he must share his hiding place with this intrusive critter. He hated spiders. "Weren't circumstances bad enough already?" he fretted.

A short time later, he heard the ominous sound of soldiers' footsteps approaching. He held his breath as one man came to the entrance of the cave, stopped briefly and then called out, "There is no use checking this place. There's a spider's web across the entrance." The voice continued, "He would have had to break it to enter. Let's move on." Whereupon, the footsteps faded away and Robert's unwelcome intruder had been the instrument that saved his life. Robert the Bruce was Scotland's best loved king, reigning from 1306 to 1329 AD. His life dream was Scotland's deliverance from England, and he lived just long enough to see it happen. He is credited with bringing about Scotland's freedom in 1328 AD, just a short time before his death.

In a slightly different approach, Erwin Lutzer, in his book "One Minute After You Die," claims that "although death might appear to be man's greatest enemy" it is actually "his great-est friend, because it is only through death that we can go to God," and we might add, live with Him in eternity.

If sickness, pain, impossible people, or a spider's web can deliver those who are under attack, can we not trust God's plan for causing *our worst enemies* to become our "*best friends*"?

"As for you, you meant evil against me; but God meant it for good." (Genesis 50:20)

Conclusion

❖

Serenity

Today I scanned - from on a hill
The world below - so small and still.
God's peace abounded there for me,
 As I tasted - touched - eternity.

CPSIA information can be obtained at www.ICGtesting.com
Printed in the USA
BVOW080643021112

304405BV00003B/2/P